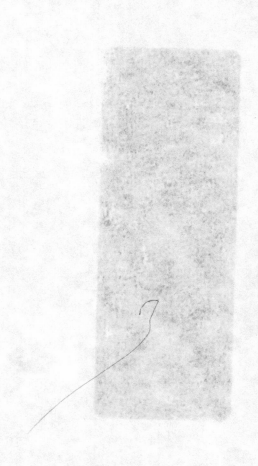

WORLD
HISTORY SERIES

Modern Japan

Titles in the World History Series

Modern Japan

by
Don Nardo

Lucent Books, P.O. Box 289011, San Diego, CA 92198-9011

Library of Congress Cataloging-in-Publication Data

Nardo, Don, 1947-
    Modern Japan / by Don Nardo.
        p. cm. — (World history series)
    Includes bibliographical references and index.
    ISBN 1-56006-281-9 (acid free)
    1. Japan—History—1868—Juvenile literature.
I. Title. II. Series.
DS881.9.N37   1995
952.03—dc20   94-26393
                                                    CIP
                                                    AC

Contents

Foreword

Each year on the first day of school, nearly every history teacher faces the task of explaining why his or her students should study history. One logical answer to this question is that exploring what happened in our past explains how the things we often take for granted—our customs, ideas, and institutions—came to be. As statesman and historian Winston Churchill put it, "Every nation or group of nations has its own tale to tell. Knowledge of the trials and struggles is necessary to all who would comprehend the problems, perils, challenges, and opportunities which confront us today." Thus, a study of history puts modern ideas and institutions in perspective. For example, though the founders of the United States were talented and creative thinkers, they clearly did not invent the concept of democracy. Instead, they adapted some democratic ideas that had originated in ancient Greece and with which the Romans, the British, and others had experimented. An exploration of these cultures, then, reveals their very real connection to us through institutions that continue to shape our daily lives.

Another reason often given for studying history is the idea that lessons exist in the past from which contemporary societies can benefit and learn. This idea, although controversial, has always been an intriguing one for historians. Those that agree that society can benefit from the past often quote philosopher George Santayana's famous statement, "Those who cannot remember the past are condemned to repeat it." Historians who ascribe to Santayana's philosophy believe that, for example, studying the events that led up to the major world wars or other significant historical events would allow society to chart a different and more favorable course in the future.

Just as difficult as convincing students to realize the importance of studying history is the search for useful and interesting supplementary materials that present historical events in a context that can be easily understood. The volumes in Lucent Books' World History Series attempt to present a broad, balanced, and penetrating view of the march of history. Ancient Egypt's important wars and rulers, for example, are presented against the rich and colorful backdrop of Egyptian religious, social, and cultural developments. The series engages the reader by enhancing historical events with these cultural contexts. For example, in *Ancient Greece*, the text covers the role of women in that society. Slavery is discussed in *The Roman Empire*, as well as how slaves earned their freedom. The numerous and varied aspects of everyday life in these and other societies are explored in each volume of the series. Additionally, the series covers the major political, cultural, and philosophical ideas as the torch of civilization is passed from ancient Mesopotamia and Egypt, through Greece, Rome, Medieval Europe, and other world cultures, to the modern day.

The material in the series is formatted in a thorough, precise, and organized manner. Each volume offers the reader a comprehensive and clearly written overview of an important historical event or period. The topic under discussion is placed in a broad, historical context. For example, *The Italian Renaissance* begins with a discussion of the High Middle Ages and the loss of central control that allowed certain Italian cities to develop artistically. The book ends by looking forward to the Reformation and interpreting the societal changes that grew out of the Renaissance. Thus, students are not only involved in an historical era, but also enveloped by the events leading up to that era and the events following it.

One important and unique feature in the World History Series is the primary and secondary source quotations that richly supplement each volume. These quotes are useful in a number of ways. First, they allow students access to sources they would not normally be exposed to because of the difficulty and obscurity of the original source. The quotations range from interesting anecdotes to far-sighted cultural perspectives and are drawn from historical witnesses both past and present. Second, the quotes demonstrate how and where historians themselves derive their information on the past as they strive to reach a consensus on historical events. Lastly, all of the quotes are footnoted, familiarizing students with the citation process and allowing them to verify quotes and/or look up the original source if the quote piques their interest.

Finally, the books in the World History Series provide a detailed launching point for further research. Each book contains a bibliography specifically geared toward student research. A second, annotated bibliography introduces students to all the sources the author consulted when compiling the book. A chronology of important dates gives students an overview, at a glance, of the topic covered. Where applicable, a glossary of terms is included.

In short, the series is designed not only to acquaint readers with the basics of history, but also to make them aware that their lives are a part of an ongoing human saga. Perhaps they will then come to the same realization as famed historian Arnold Toynbee. In his monumental work, *A Study of History,* he wrote about becoming aware of history flowing through him in a mighty current, and of his own life "welling like a wave in the flow of this vast tide."

Important Dates in Modern Japanese History

| 1603 | 1850 | 1860 | 1870 | 1880 | 1890 | 1900 | 1910 |

1603
Tokugawa Ieyasu establishes the Tokugawa shogunate

1641
Japan is effectively isolated from the rest of the world

1853
U.S. warships under Commodore Perry arrive in Japan and intimidate the Japanese

1854
Japan and the United States sign the Treaty of Kanagawa, opening Japan to the outside world

1863
Statesman Ito Hirobumi travels to Europe to learn about Western customs and governments

1867
A rebellion causes the fall of the Tokugawa government

1868
Japan's new leaders announce the Meiji Restoration, or "return to imperial rule"; Tokyo becomes the new capital and the country begins a massive modernization program

1871
The leaders abolish the old Tokugawa class system, making all Japanese citizens equal under the law

1872
Japan's first railway line, linking Tokyo and Yokohama, is completed; military leader Yamagata Aritomo introduces universal military conscription

1877
Former government official Saigo Takamori leads an unsuccessful rebellion against the government

1889
The emperor grants a new constitution, drafted by Ito Hirobumi, which establishes the Diet, a national assembly composed of two legislative houses

1894–1895
Japan fights and wins the first Sino-Japanese War with China

1898
The Japanese are outraged when Russia occupies Manchuria, a part of China

1902
Japan and Britain sign the Anglo-Japanese Alliance, designed to contain Russian ambitions in East Asia

1904–1905
Japan defeats Russia in the Russo-Japanese War, concluded with the Treaty of Portsmouth

1910
Japan annexes Korea without opposition

1912
Emperor Meiji dies, symbolically ending Japan's first modern era

1915
Japan presents China with the Twenty-One Demands, designed to expand Japanese interests in East Asia

1919
Japan is one of the "Big Five" powers at the Versailles Peace Conference officially ending World War I; writer Kita Ikki advocates that Japan move toward fascism

1921–1922
The Western nations force Japan to agree to limit its naval power at the Washington Conference

1923
A major earthquake destroys half of Tokyo and kills more than 130,000 people

1925
All adult Japanese males receive the right to vote

1931
Acting without the knowledge of the civilian government in Japan, the Japanese army in Manchuria attacks the Chinese city of Mukden

1932
The Japanese transform Manchuria into Manchukuo, a Japanese puppet state; the United States refuses to recognize Manchukuo and pledges friendship to China

| 1920 | 1930 | 1940 | 1950 | 1960 | 1970 | 1980 | 1993 |

1936
Japanese militarists launch a wave of attacks on the country's liberals, effectively giving the militarists a controlling influence in Japan's affairs

1937
Japan attacks China once more, igniting the second Sino-Japanese War

1940
The United States places an oil embargo on Japan; Tojo Hideki becomes Japan's most powerful leader

1941
The Japanese launch a surprise attack on the U.S. naval base at Pearl Harbor in Hawaii, initiating the Pacific theater of World War II; the Japanese also strike the Americans in the Philippines and attack Singapore, Hong Kong, and other British colonies in Southeast Asia

1942
The Japanese capture 130,000 British troops in Singapore, the greatest land victory in Japanese history; Japanese forces suffer a major defeat by the U.S. Navy in the Battle of Midway fought near Hawaii, an event that halts Japan's Pacific expansion

1944
Thousands of defeated Japanese commit suicide on Saipan as the Pacific island becomes one of many Japanese strongholds to fall to American forces

1945
U.S. bombers create a firestorm that kills 200,000 in Tokyo; the Americans drop atomic bombs on Hiroshima and Nagasaki, killing more than 300,000; the Japanese surrender, ending the war; the Americans, with Gen. Douglas MacArthur as supreme commander, occupy Japan

1946
The Americans initiate sweeping land reforms; Japan's first postwar elections are held

1947
A new Japanese constitution, drafted by the Americans, goes into effect

1952
Japan and the Allies gather in San Francisco and sign a peace treaty officially ending the state of war between them and recognizing Japan's sovereignty as a nation

1955
The Liberal Democratic Party comes to power in Japan

1956
Japan joins the United Nations; the Japanese government establishes the Science and Technology Agency to promote the use of modern technology in the nation's industry

1960
Japanese citizens take part in mass street demonstrations against the signing of a treaty renewing the U.S. role as Japan's protector

1964
The Japanese host the Summer Olympics in Tokyo

1968
Japan becomes the third largest industrial power in the world after the United States and the Soviet Union

1970
The Japanese host the International Exposition in Osaka

1972
U.S.-Japanese relations improve somewhat as the United States gives up control of the island of Okinawa

1993
After 38 years in power, the Japanese Liberal Democratic Party is defeated by forces led by Morihiro Hosokawa, who becomes the new prime minister

The Quest to Be Number One

The Japanese have always been strivers for excellence. Throughout their long history, both Japanese leaders and the people as a whole have placed a high priority on remaining self-sufficient, enterprising, and prosperous. And they have done so with the idea that they are unique in the world. Part of their national consciousness is a feeling that the Japanese remain separate from other peoples, and they take deep pride in that separateness. Though they have rarely said so openly, many Japanese feel just a bit more industrious, hardworking, and, therefore, deserving of success than others. Describing Japanese pride in themselves and their nation, scholar and former U.S. ambassador to Japan Edwin O. Reischauer states:

> The strength of the Japanese feeling of separateness becomes more clear-cut when one considers Japanese attitudes toward other peoples. Japanese seem to have a sharp awareness at all times of themselves as being Japanese and of others as being first of all "not Japanese." Such attitudes are hard to measure, but the Japanese seem to feel them more strongly than do other peoples. . . . The first answer of a

Priests and others participate in a procession in one of the several yearly Japanese Shinto festivals that celebrate the cycles of nature.

Japanese to the question "Who are you?" is likely to be "A Japanese."[1]

Reischauer credits this separatist attitude to several historical and cultural factors that have made Japan distinct from both Western and Eastern nations. For instance, unlike English, French, and German, which are based on older tongues, such as Latin, the Japanese language did not develop from an older language. Also, throughout its early history Japan was geographically isolated from other major cultural centers and virtually inaccessible by their representatives. So the Japanese developed many ideas and customs on their own with little outside influence. Even in modern times Japan's position is unique, says Reischauer, "as the one major industrialized country that is not of western cultural background or the white race—the country that does not quite fit into either the western or eastern worlds."[2]

Given this sense of being unique and separate, the Japanese have traditionally felt that they needed to "make it" on their own, that they could not rely on others to help guarantee their success. So the Japanese have nearly always maintained a very native and personalized way of doing things. For example, when they borrowed ideas from the outside, most often from China, they altered these ideas to fit Japanese molds. The result was that the borrowed concepts and institutions became uniquely Japanese in character. More importantly, strong feelings of national pride instilled the belief that the Japanese versions were somehow better, improved, more efficient, or more virtuous. A prime example was the way the early Japanese borrowed Buddhist religious doctrine from China and combined it with traditional Japanese Shinto beliefs. Most Japanese preferred the resulting hybrid faith to the Chinese original.

The Japanese quest to achieve and maintain a special and unique status continued in modern times. In the late nineteenth century, Japan, then a militarily and economically backward country, underwent a profound transformation. One goal was to become equal to Western nations such as the United States, Britain, and Russia. Another goal was to make Japan the number-one power and cultural center of the East Asian sphere.

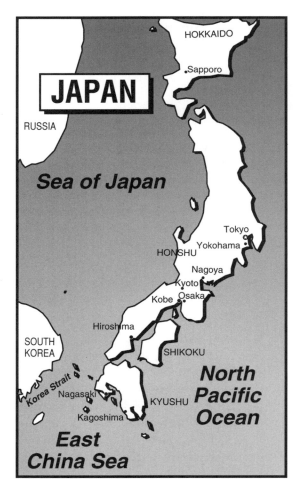

This busy Tokyo marketplace is just one example of the overall economic prosperity that Japan has enjoyed in the second half of the twentieth century.

The Japanese accomplished these goals and then, in the 1930s and 1940s, attempted through military aggression to establish dominance over an even wider area. Japan's bid for world domination (along with its allies Germany and Italy) failed when the country suffered defeat and devastation at the end of World War II.

But even this disastrous defeat did not spell the end of Japanese expressions of individualism and national achievement. In the second half of the twentieth century, Japan channeled its considerable energies into the financial sphere and rose to prominence as an economic giant. The new goal was once more domination—in this case over world markets. As scholar Edward J. Lincoln points out, in the 1990s the Japanese are not far from actually fulfilling this lofty objective:

> Japan is both a major trading nation and one of the largest international investors in the world. In many respects, international trade is the lifeblood of Japan's economy, and it is the window through which most people in the United States view Japan. Imports and exports totaling the equivalent of US$452 billion in 1988 meant that Japan was the world's third largest trading nation after the United States and [Germany] . . . giving Japan new world prominence.[3]

Whether the Japanese will someday become number one in world financial matters is impossible to say. Some experts, such as Asian affairs scholar Ezra Vogel in his 1979 book *Japan as Number One*, have taken the view that the Japanese will inevitably control the world's economy. Others believe this scenario is unlikely. "Like all stereotypes, this one was never true," says financial expert Robert J. Samuelson in a December 1993 *Newsweek* editorial titled "Japan as Number Two." But even doubters like Samuelson concede that the Japanese have achieved a phenomenal degree of economic success, mainly through the application of good old-fashioned values. "The main ingredients of Japan's success are not novel," Samuelson states; they are "hard work, good management and productive investment."[4] Indeed, these ingredients, especially hard work, have always been the forces driving Japanese efficiency and success. The open question remains whether such forces will in the coming century propel the Japanese to their age-old goal of being number one.

1 Japan's Incredible Transformation: The Meiji Restoration

July 8, 1853, marked one of the great turning points in Japanese history. On that fateful day a squadron of four U.S. warships moved silently and ominously into Edo (now Tokyo) Bay on the eastern coast of Honshu, the largest and most populous of the more than four thousand islands that make up the nation of Japan. Thousands of people lined the shores to catch a glimpse, their first ever close up, of the dreaded foreign "black ships" that had for centuries remained vague and mysterious dots on the far horizon.

An engraving depicts the vessels of U.S. commodore Perry's fateful 1853 expedition to Japan.

Ending a Long Isolation

Indeed, the vast majority of Japanese had never seen a foreigner and knew nothing of what was happening in the outside world. A handful of Dutch traders were allowed marginal visits on a single island but had no contact with Japanese society as a whole. Since the early 1600s, the Tokugawa, the family that controlled the *bakufu*, Japan's military government, had kept the country isolated from most foreigners. The supreme commanders, or shoguns, maintained that the "corrupt" ideas and customs of the foreign "barbarians" might pollute Japanese society. So the Japanese lacked modern technology, such as trains, steam engines, telescopes, and cotton gins.

Not surprisingly then, the huge steam-powered vessels entering Edo Bay seemed strange and threatening to those who watched from shore. Far larger than any Japanese ships, the American boats were bristling with massive cannon and other armaments that clearly could, if provoked, reduce the great city of Edo to ruins. And in fact, the American display of armed might was fully intended to intimidate the Japanese. The fleet's commander, Commodore Matthew Perry, had

Commodore Perry presents the Tokugawa shogun with President Millard Fillmore's letters, which demand that Japan open trade relations with the United States.

been ordered by the U.S. government to open Japan to the outside world by any means necessary, including force. According to Edwin Reischauer:

> In the first half of the nineteenth century the Americans, English, and Russians repeatedly sent expeditions to Japan in an effort to persuade the Japanese to open their ports to foreign ships, and the Dutch urged the Tokugawa to accede [give in] to these demands. But Edo stood firm on its old policy. . . . The vast majority of the people, long accustomed to isolation from the rest of the world, were bitterly opposed to allowing foreigners into their land. It was obvious that Japan would not voluntarily open her doors. The American government eventually decided to try to force the doors open.[5]

Commodore Perry and his officers were both confused and impressed by the reception they received in Edo. They were confused because they had heard that Japan was ruled by an emperor, and they had letters addressed to him from President Millard Fillmore. Yet the shogun and his office, the shogunate, seemed to be the real power in the country. The Americans soon learned that the emperor was merely a figurehead. For the moment, the shogun's deputies decided to avoid a confrontation with the Americans by reluctantly but politely receiving the letters. What impressed Perry and his men was that the Japanese, despite their lack of modern technology, seemed so civilized and culturally refined. The Americans had expected to encounter a much cruder and less advanced society. In the months and years ahead, Western scholars would learn that the Japanese possessed a rich and varied history, one older and in many ways more complex than those of many Western nations. It became clear that Japanese achievements in nation building, religious philosophy, art, architecture, and literature easily rivaled those in the West.

Over the Mists of Time

As early as A.D. 300, there existed on Honshu a culture advanced enough to build houses, towns, and ships, and to practice large-scale agriculture. Pockets of this tribal society also existed on some of the other larger Japanese islands, principally Kyushu and Shikoku, lying south of Honshu. Inhabiting a fourth large island, Hokkaido, directly north of Honshu, was a less advanced people known as the Ainu.

Jimmu, Japan's first emperor. According to Japanese tradition, he was descended from the sun goddess Amaterasu.

Individual Japanese towns and villages were ruled by strong male family heads, who gave allegiance to a line of emperors. According to tradition, the line originated in 660 B.C. when Japan, the "land of the rising sun," was founded by Jimmu, the first emperor. Jimmu's own heritage was said to stretch back over the mists of time directly to Amaterasu, the sun goddess, Japan's patron and most revered deity. This was the basis of the belief, which lingered well into modern times, that as direct descendants of the goddess, the Japanese emperors were semidivine beings.

But while the emperors remained respected and revered, they eventually lost most of the political power they once may have wielded. They became largely figureheads in whose name the men with real power ruled. These rulers, important members of prominent families, were always careful to get the support of the emperor for any new decision or policy. In the eyes of the Japanese people, who were very religious and tradition oriented, only those leaders who enjoyed the blessings of the emperor were legitimate.

In time, a few of the most powerful families formed large and powerful clans, called *uji*. The leaders of these clans constituted a privileged aristocracy that attended the imperial court and vied for the emperor's favor. The first known *uji* to gain great power and prestige was the Soga clan. Beginning in about A.D. 530, the Soga held sway over the rich Yamato Plain in south-central Honshu, an area that quickly became the most populous and culturally developed region of the country. Thereafter, Japanese politics and court life, always centered in Yamato, came to be dominated by one powerful family after another. For instance, after about a century the Soga gave way to the Fujiwara, who, after ruling for more than four centuries, lost power to the Taira and Minamoto.

The Succession of the Great Families

Each successive great family left its mark on Japanese society. The Soga's principal legacy was the introduction of Buddhism to Japan. The Buddhist faith, which had originated in India and China, consists of a series of "right" behaviors aimed at making people's lives and the world more harmonious and peaceful. The Japanese

Each year, tens of thousands of Japanese visit this huge and very old bronze statue of Buddha in the Japanese town of Kamakura.

never borrowed a foreign idea outright, however. They combined Buddhist doctrine with their native Shinto religion, which consisted of prayer to traditional ancient gods like Amaterasu and nature spirits known as *kami*. Thus, like the country's other cultural aspects, Japanese Buddhism had a uniquely ethnic character. "One of the most intriguing features of the Japanese people," says historian W. Scott Morton, "is their capacity to borrow and adapt and yet to retain their own individuality and their own style."[6]

The contributions of the Fujiwara were profound. They established the country's first capital and first true city in 710 at Nara in central Yamato. In 794 the capital moved to Heian, later called Kyoto, where it remained until the nineteenth century. Under Fujiwara rule, art and literature thrived. Among the great literary works produced were the *Kojiki* (712) and the *Nihongi* (720), collections of ancient creation myths and history; the *Tale of Genji* (1008), a colorful depiction of imperial court life and the world's first novel; and tens of thousands of descriptive diaries and poems. The Fujiwara also fought and defeated the Ainu, who had been raiding farms in northern Honshu.

The rule of the Minamoto marked the rise of militarism in Japan. In 1185, after defeating rival clans, Minamoto Yoritomo founded the first military *bakufu*, which means "tent government." (Japanese family names come first, followed by given names. Although it is customary to designate historical figures by given name after the family name has been mentioned once, many modern figures are referred to by their family names after their given names have been mentioned.) Yoritomo took the title of shogun, or supreme military general.

His rule also marked the beginnings of feudalism in Japan. As the feudal system evolved, powerful regional lords known as *daimyo* held large estates on which poor peasants worked the land, and each lord policed his realm with his own private army of warriors, called samurai. Similar in many ways to medieval European knights, the samurai swore allegiance to their lord and protected his interests in return for a share of his land and its bounty. The lord, in turn, swore allegiance to the shogun, who also received a share of the bounty from each estate.

The samurai lived by a strict code of honor called *bushido* and were expected to commit *seppuku* (also known as hara-kiri), a gruesome form of ritual suicide, rather than live with disgrace or dishonor. That the samurai class rose when it did turned out to be fortunate for Japan. In 1274 and 1281, the Mongols, a warlike people from the Asian mainland, invaded Japan. The fighting skills and heroism of the samurai kept the enemy at bay until the Mongol fleet was destroyed in a great storm. The Japanese attributed their salvation to the

Samurai warriors in their traditional robes and carrying samurai swords, as they appeared in the eighteenth and nineteenth centuries.

Japanese warriors fight the Mongols on the beaches of western Kyushu during the great Mongol invasion of 1274.

gods, whom they believed had sent the *kamikaze*, or "divine wind." The concept of the *kamikaze* would again become a factor in Japanese warfare, with devastating results, in modern times.

In time, other strong and influential families, including the Hojo and the Ashikaga, rose to control Japanese affairs. During the reign of the Ashikaga shoguns, from the late 1300s to the mid-1500s, feudalism became less centralized. The *daimyo* controlled the countryside as the shogunate became weak and ineffective. The result was constant civil strife and political anarchy. Then, in 1542, the first Europeans arrived in Japan. Portuguese traders introduced guns and castle building, innovations that had a profound effect on the country. Combining these tools with their own considerable talents, three strong and capable leaders rose. In the final decades of the sixteenth century, Oda Nobunaga, Toyotomi Hideyoshi, and Tokugawa Ieyasu managed to unite the various *daimyo*, regions, and islands into a true Japanese nation with a strong central *bakufu* once more in charge.

Japan in Isolation

In 1603 Ieyasu established the Tokugawa shogunate, which maintained complete control of Japan for the next two and a half centuries. The Tokugawa were worried about increasing foreign influences in the country, especially the rapid spread of Christianity, which seemed to pose a threat to traditional religious and social values. The Tokugawa leaders reacted with harsh and extreme measures. They launched massive and brutal persecutions that all but wiped out the Japanese Christians. They also expelled all foreigners from the country, with the exception of a few Dutch traders. By 1641, Japan was effectively isolated from the rest of the world. During this self-imposed isolation, the Japanese focused all their attention and energies inward. Many large cities rose, local crafts and trading thrived, and literature and the arts flourished. The people reaffirmed ancient teachings that advocated the superiority of Japan over

Commodore Perry meets with representatives of the shogun and the emperor in Yokohama in 1853. Perry himself was dignified and treated the Japanese politely. Yet he was also firm in his demands and did not hesitate to warn the Japanese about the superior armaments the United States possessed.

Conquest in God's Name

When increasing numbers of Western ships began to appear in Japanese waters in the 1820s, Japan's leaders perceived a crisis that might threaten the country's isolation. So they sanctioned writings that reaffirmed the goodness of Japanese ways and warned of the evil natures of the "barbarians." One such writing was this 1825 tract by Aizawa Seishisai, quoted here from Sources of Japanese Tradition, *edited by William T. de Bary.*

"The western barbarians have independent and mutually contending states [countries], but they all follow the same God. When there is something to be gained by it, they get together in order to achieve their aims and share the benefits. But when trouble is brewing, each stays within its own boundaries for self-protection. So when there is trouble in the west, the east generally enjoys peace. But when the trouble has quieted down, they go out to ravage other lands in all directions and then the east becomes a sufferer. . . . As to the western barbarians who have dominated the seas for nearly three centuries—do they surpass others in intelligence and bravery? . . . Are their social institutions and administration of justice perfect in every detail? . . . Not so at all. All that they have is Christianity to fall back upon in the prosecution of their schemes. . . . When those barbarians plan to subdue a country not their own, they start by opening commerce and watch for a sign of weakness. If an opportunity is presented, they will preach their alien religion to captivate the people's hearts. Once the people's allegiance has been shifted, they can be manipulated and nothing can be done to stop it. . . . The subversion of the people and overthrowing of the state are taught as being in accord with the God's will. So in the name of all-embracing love [of God] the subjugation [conquest] of the land is accomplished. Though greed is the real motive, it masquerades as a righteous uprising. The absorption of the country and conquest of its territories are all done in this fashion."

other nations, and the idea that foreigners were barbarians to be feared and shunned was encouraged.

It was with this attitude of extreme wariness and distrust that the Japanese greeted Commodore Perry's expedition in 1853. In an effort to display Japanese resolve and readiness to resist American hostility, the *bakufu* ordered five thousand troops to surround the building in which

Perry met with Tokugawa representatives. But this attempted show of force did not impress Perry, who was well aware that his military advantage was vastly superior. He wasted no time in demanding that the Japanese open their ports to American trade and allow U.S. military and whaling vessels to resupply themselves in Japan. Perry added that if these "very reasonable and pacific [peaceful] overtures" were not accepted, he would return the following year "with a much larger force."[7] To make sure that his meaning was clear, in the next two days Perry ordered his warships, their cannon facing the shore, to sail menacingly around Edo Bay.

Perry gave the Japanese until the following spring to make up their minds. Although popular opinion was strongly for rejecting the demands and standing up to the United States, the Tokugawa realized that their forces were no match for American military might. So in 1854 the *bakufu* leaders gave in and signed the Treaty of Kanagawa with the United States. After this, the outside world relentlessly closed in on Japan. As Edwin Reischauer puts it:

> Once the door had been pushed open a crack, there was no closing it. Within two years Edo had signed treaties with England, Russia, and Holland, and in 1858 Townsend Harris, the first American consul, negotiated a full commercial treaty, including the unequal provision that Americans would enjoy extraterritoriality in Japan, that is, the right to be tried by their own consular courts, as had become the practice in western treaty relations with China. The European powers soon made similar treaties with Japan, and the door was now wide open.[8]

A Bold and Unprecedented Strategy

The weakness shown by the *bakufu* in backing down to the Western nations provoked severe criticism of the government, and eventually violent opposition. During the 1860s, Tokugawa power and prestige steadily declined as a number of powerful *daimyo* tried to gain influence over the imperial court. Clearly, it was essential to get the emperor's backing before attempting to seize power from the *bakufu*. This period of political struggle is sometimes referred to as the *bakumatsu*, or "end of the *bakufu*." Late in 1867 the defiant *daimyo* launched a brief but bloody rebellion that

Tokugawa Kei-Ki, the last Tokugawa shogun, as he appeared in his ornate court robes shortly before being overthrown in 1867.

succeeded in overthrowing the Tokugawa. The triumphant lords abolished the *bakufu* and formed a ruling coalition from among their own ranks.

The new leaders now faced choosing a fresh course for the country. But at first they were unsure of which course to take. To reassure a worried populace and also to solidify their own power, in January 1868 they called upon all Japanese to unite behind the emperor, who would, for the first time in many centuries, assume a measure of real authority. The fifteen-year-old emperor Mutsuhito took the reign title of Meiji, meaning "enlightened rule," and the supposed return to imperial rule became known as the Meiji Restoration. This was a ploy, however, for the new leaders fully intended to make all the important decisions themselves and keep the emperor a figurehead. Since the term "oligarchy" refers to rule by an elite group of individuals, historians often call the lords who now controlled both the emperor and the Japanese state the Meiji oligarchy.

The first important decision to be made revolved around the foreigners and their intimidating demands on Japan. The members of the oligarchy soberly observed the spread of Western imperialism in Asia. Through the use of threats and force, Britain, the United States, Russia, and others were steadily gaining military and economic dominance over China, Korea, and other East Asian lands. Rather than submit to the same fate, the new Japanese leaders decided on a bold and unprecedented strategy. In their view, the best course was to initiate a massive modernization program, one that would eventually make Japan both militarily and economically equal to the Western powers, perhaps even superior. They fully real-

The young emperor Mutsuhito, who assumed the title of Meiji in 1868, became a symbol of Japan's new modern state.

ized that the necessary changes would affect all levels and aspects of society, sweeping away many long-held traditions and institutions. But they believed there was no other way for Japan to become a great independent nation. Thus, 1868 marked a major turning point: traditional Japan ended, and the country's incredible transformation into a modern state began.

Building the New Japan

To help dramatize the "new order" they planned for the nation, the oligarchs moved the capital from Kyoto to Edo, the country's largest city, which they renamed Tokyo, or "eastern capital." They promised that a first step in building the new Japan would be to replace the "evil customs" of the past with the "just laws of nature." To this end, they issued the Charter Oath, a sort of sketchy preliminary constitution, in April 1868. One article of the oath stated that assemblies of citizens would eventually be allowed to discuss and decide public policy, seemingly a move toward democracy. But in reality, only powerful and influential individuals would have a say in national affairs. The oligarchy was merely trying to gain the support of many regional *daimyo* who thus far felt left out of the political process.

Other articles of the Charter Oath were more substantial and held more real potential for changing society. For example, Article 3 stated: "The common people, no less than civil and military officials, shall each be allowed to pursue his own calling so that there may be no discontent."[9] According to W. Scott Morton:

> This was a promise that the frustrating class barriers of feudalism would no longer be in force and that all careers would be open to those with talent. The whole country, in fact, would become a man-power pool for the immense effort of modernization.[10]

Class System Abolished

The oligarchy kept this promise. In 1871 it abolished the old Tokugawa class system, which strictly designated those who would be lords, samurai, farmers, artisans, or merchants. Under the new system, everyone was, at least theoretically, equal under the law. In reality many class distinctions remained. For instance, the former *daimyo* soon became a kind of nobility based on the European system of dukes, earls, and barons. But on the whole, a real and far-reaching reordering of many social ranks took place. The samurai were affected more than most, losing their exclusive claim to military positions. Some former warriors did remain military officers, but most became teachers, bankers, scholars, police officials, and journalists.

Equally significant was Article 5 of the Charter Oath, which called for modernizing and strengthening the country by seeking scientific, industrial, economic, and legal knowledge from all parts of the world. According to historian Robert L. Worden:

> The Meiji oligarchy was aware of western progress, and "learning missions" were sent abroad to absorb as much of it as possible. One such mission, led by [oligarchy members] Iwakura, Kido, and Okubo, and containing forty-eight members in total, spent two years (1871–1873) touring the United States and Europe, studying government institutions, courts, prison systems, schools, the import-export business, factories, shipyards, glass plants, mines, and other enterprises. Upon returning, mission members called for domestic reforms that would help Japan catch up with the west.[11]

Thanks to this knowledge gathered from abroad and also to the zeal with which the government pushed its reforms, Japan began with meteoric speed to close the gap that separated it from the modern industrial nations. The government financed massive building programs that included warships, harbors, lighthouses, factories, roads, railroads, and telegraph networks. A typical example of the rapid

The Emperor Meiji officially opens the Tokyo-Yokohama line, Japan's first usable stretch of railway, in 1872.

progress of these programs was railroad construction. A short railway link between Tokyo and Yokohama, located a few miles southwest of the capital, was completed in 1872, and by 1880 it was carrying two million passengers a year. In 1881 Japan had some 76 miles of usable track laid. By 1885, the total had increased to 350 miles and by 1895 to an astonishing 2,080 miles. Similarly spectacular was the increase in the number of individual spindles for making cloth in modern-style textile mills. There were only 8,000 spindles in 1877, but more than 382,000 spindles by 1893.

Reaction to Change

Other changes instigated by the government affected people in some of the simplest aspects of their daily lives. One important example was the introduction of a new calendar on January 1, 1873. Historian W. G. Beasley explains:

> The Gregorian calendar, as used in western Europe . . . replaced the lunar calendar originally derived from China. The change affected much that was familiar. Dates for festivals, the beginning of the four seasons, the New Year itself, all now fell on different days. The farmer had to learn new designations for his times of planting and harvesting, the merchant for his debt-collecting, the priest for his ceremonials. Even though many preferred to go on using the old system side by side with the new, the decision had repercussions [consequences] which struck deep into Japanese life. Equally, it symbolized an important aspect of the government's policy, its determination

to turn away from the traditional and towards the modern, away from China and towards the west.[12]

It is hardly surprising that after so many centuries of largely unchanging traditions, some Japanese were unhappy with so many jarring and sudden changes. Most of the discontented citizens grudgingly did their best to adjust, but a few were willing to use forceful means to turn the clock of progress backwards. Among these reactionaries was Saigo Takamori, one of the original Meiji oligarchs. After serious disagreements with his colleagues over foreign policy, Saigo resigned from the government in 1873 and returned to his home on Kyushu. He built a chain of military schools that promoted the old samurai *bushido* ideals, and eventually his students numbered as many as twenty thousand. Several former lords and samurai, unhappy with the Meiji reforms, joined forces with these students and persuaded Saigo to lead them against the government. In 1877 about forty thousand rebels attempted to march on Tokyo.

But the government forces that opposed them had more men, modern weapons, and a much larger supply base. Within six months, the rebellion was crushed and Saigo committed suicide, ending serious physical threats to the Meiji regime.

Demands for Democratic Reform

Some opposition to the oligarchy remained, however, in the form of increasing verbal and written petitions demanding that the people have a greater say in government. Many Japanese had taken the framers of the Charter Oath at their word when they had promised a move toward democratic institutions. In 1874 Itakagi Taisuke, an influential politician, established the country's first political party, the *Aikoku Koto*, or Public Society of Patriots. The party and other groups and individuals eventually persuaded members of the oligarchy to agree to a slow phase-in of

Government police forces march through Tokyo on their way to put down the 1877 rebellion led by former Meiji oligarch Saigo Takamori.

The Rise of a Statesman

Ito Hirobumi (1841–1909), who drafted the 1889 constitution, was one of Japan's most important early modern statesmen. In this excerpt from his book Japan: A Concise History, *historian Milton W. Meyer cites Ito's rise to prominence.*

"Of lowly Choshu [clan] samurai background, Ito rose through a hierarchical society [one having positions of authority ranked in increasingly higher steps] to pinnacles of power. As a youth he had a vigorous induction into *bushido*, the code of the warrior. From his teachers, among whom was Yoshida Shoin [who advocated borrowing selected ideas from the West], he inherited strong traits of self-discipline and loyalty. He also was impressed with the necessity of acquiring western knowledge. In 1863, he went to Europe on an English ship, and on his return he became . . . a leading Choshu advocate of coming to terms with the west. After the [Meiji] restoration, he rose to become an important member of the inner government oligarchy. His first appointment was in the new Bureau of Foreign Affairs, and he later moved on to become minister of finance and industry, and, finally, to the prime ministership. In 1870, a second mission to the west included a stay in the United States. During 1882–1884, Ito made a third trip to the west as the head of an imperial commission to study constitutions. He was particularly impressed by [Chancellor Otto von] Bismarck's new Germany, which resembled Japan in some ways."

Statesman Ito Hirobumi made several trips to Western nations and advocated adopting Western ideas and technology.

democratic forms. In 1879 Japan's prefectures, or individual provinces, were allowed to form local assemblies, although these had very limited powers. Another limiting factor was a narrow franchise, or right to vote. The only people who could vote were male adults having a certain financial means, a group constituting a tiny minority of the population.

Nevertheless, champions of democracy persevered and won more concessions from the government. In 1881 the oligarchy declared that an official constitution would be drawn up, with a national assembly to be established by 1890. Statesman Ito Hirobumi, who had toured Europe in 1863, drafted the new constitution, which the emperor bestowed on the people as a royal gift on February 11, 1889. The document provided for a legislative assembly called the Diet, similar in some ways to Britain's Parliament. The Diet had two houses. The ministers of the upper house, the House of Peers, were members of the nobility or the emperor's special appointees and served for life. The lower house, the House of Representatives, had three hundred popularly elected ministers, who had set terms of service.

The Diet could approve some government legislation, mainly budget related, and it could initiate some laws. But unlike Britain's Parliament, the Japanese assembly was far from being a democratic body. Under the new constitution, only about 1 percent of the population were allowed to vote: namely, male adults who paid 15 yen (the basic monetary unit) or more a year in taxes. Also, real power still rested in the hands of the oligarchs and their puppet emperor. Japan remained basically an authoritarian state, ruled by an elite.

Satisfying government critics by giving the people what amounted to the illusion of democracy only served to solidify the power of the oligarchs, who soon became known as the *genro*, or "elder statesmen." They now had little opposition to their continuing effort to transform the country into a world power. Having for years concentrated their energies on the first step—unifying and modernizing Japan—

The emperor solemnly opens the Diet's first session in 1889. Although the national assembly had some legislative powers, it was overshadowed by the oligarchs, who held the country's real power.

The Emperor's Ultimate Authority

On February 15, 1889, a few days after the emperor had granted the new constitution, Ito Hirobumi, who had drafted the document, made a speech, from which this excerpt (quoted in Sources of Japanese Tradition*) is taken.*

"Our Constitution consists of seven chapters and seventy-six articles, and as you have probably read and re-read it carefully, there is no need now to discuss it article by article. Let me, therefore, take this occasion to compare our Constitution with those of other countries. The differences between our Constitution and their constitutions are considerable. For example, Chapter I which clarifies sovereignty [ultimate authority] . . . has no parallel in the constitutions of other countries. The reason for this difference can be understood at a moment's reflection. Our country was founded and ruled by the emperor himself since the very beginning of our history. Thus, to state this fact in the opening article of the Constitution is truly compatible with our national polity [organized society]. . . . In Europe . . . [scholars] advanced the theory of separation of powers. Separation of powers . . . is the division of the three powers of legislation, justice, and administration into three independent organs. However, according to a theory based on careful study and on actual experience [perhaps in Germany] . . . sovereignty is one and indivisible. It is like the human body which has limbs and bones but whose source of spiritual life is the mind. . . . That this theory coincides with our interpretation of sovereignty [giving ultimate power to the emperor] is significant."

these men would soon initiate the second step. The *genro* saw clearly that one key to the success of the Western powers was their control and exploitation of weaker foreign lands. Japan could not become great, they reasoned, unless it did the same. Aggressive domestic policy would henceforth have its counterpart in aggressive foreign policy, as leaders of the late nineteenth century prepared to steer the nation down the bold and dangerous path of expansionism.

2 An Awakening Giant: Early Japanese Expansion

As the Meiji Restoration continued in the last years of the nineteenth century and first years of the twentieth century, Japan began a concerted policy of expansionism. The Japanese government, led by the aging *genro*, used the Western style of imperialism as a model. With the continuing goal of making Japan a world power, they expanded the country's influence on the Asian mainland and in other areas of the East Asian and Pacific spheres. Disputes over Korea, the Asian peninsula lying only about one hundred miles off Japan's western shores, and Manchuria, the Chinese province located north and west of Korea, led to wars with both China and Russia. The results of these conflicts partly achieved the *genro*'s main goal by establishing Japan as the dominant East Asian power.

Japanese leaders had no qualms about using the undisguised aggressive tactics of imperialism. If the Western powers could consistently get away with dominating other countries, they reasoned, why not the Japanese? Anyway, such aggressive policies seemed essential to building up Japan's economy and defenses. In his book *Japan: Past and Present*, Edwin Reischauer explains:

During the second half of the nineteenth century, the European powers were engaged in a mad scramble to build up colonial empires by carving out new domains in Africa, Asia, and Oceania [the Pacific region]. Overseas expansion and colonial possessions were the mark of a successful power. Japanese leaders, with their samurai backgrounds, enthusiastically embraced the current imperialism of Europe and soon outstripped the western imperialists in their determination to win colonies. They saw that poor and small Japan needed more natural resources to become a first-class world power, and they believed that control of adjacent territories would yield many of these resources and strengthen the defenses of Japan. The political decay and military weakness of China and Korea made these lands ripe for foreign aggression.[13]

Building Up the Military

One important reason for the effectiveness of the program of military expansion launched by the Japanese was that during the Meiji period the rulers had concentrated on building a modern army and navy. In 1872, shortly after the oligarchy had established the Navy Ministry, the country had only seventeen warships. All but two of these were old-fashioned wooden vessels. After two decades of vigorous naval expansion, however, Japan possessed a fleet of twenty-eight modern ironclad warships plus twenty-four small but deadly torpedo boats. The nation also had several large modern dockyards for repairs and maintenance.

Just as impressive was the reorganization of the army accomplished by the talented military leader Yamagata Aritomo. In the 1870s, Yamagata completely overhauled the army ranks, using the efficient German army as a model. He created a general staff of highly trained officers, many of whom were former samurai. In 1872 he introduced a system of universal conscription in which young Japanese men were called up for military service. "Where there is a state," he declared, "there is military defense; and if there is military defense there must be military service. It follows, therefore, that the law providing for a militia is the law of nature and not an accidental, man-made law."[14]

According to scholar William T. de Bary, the idea of nationwide conscription was bold at the time because it did not sit well with the former samurai class:

For the modern reader it may be difficult to appreciate how radical an innovator Yamagata's introduction of conscription in 1872 made him. What we take for granted as an almost inevitable part of national defense was for Japan at the time not only a striking change in the military establishment

The Japanese flag, depicting the "rising sun" symbolizing the nation, dominates this photo of a Japanese naval fleet in the early 1900s. In only a few decades, the Japanese produced a modern navy comparable to those of the Western powers.

Military leader Yamagata Aritomo, who forged Japan's first and very effective modern army in the late 1800s. His prime model was the German army, the most efficient in Europe.

twelve years. This allowed him to maintain a peacetime force of 73,000 men and a wartime call-up of 200,000 men available on short notice. By 1894, all were equipped with modern rifles and field artillery comparable to the ordnance used by the major Western powers. Yamagata's new system made the army, and with it the country, much stronger than either had ever been.

A Swift and Overwhelming Victory

The first major test of this new military strength came in 1894. Japan and China hotly disagreed about the status of Korea, over which the Chinese had claimed suzerainty for some time. Suzerainty is a relationship between two countries in which the stronger dominates and controls the weaker while allowing it to manage its own domestic affairs. Korea had been a long-standing sore spot for the Japanese. Ever since the Mongol invasions of the thirteenth century, they had referred to the nearby Korean peninsula as "an arrow pointed at the heart of Japan." "Since the Korean peninsula was so close to us geographically," explains Japanese historian Oka Yoshitake, "its domination by a third party was regarded as a great threat to our national independence."[16] For centuries, Japan had periodically tried to extend its influence over Korea, hoping not only to remove any immediate threat to the home islands, but also to give the Japanese new farmlands and natural resources. None of these early attempts to solve the "Korean problem" had been successful, however.

but a virtual social revolution. The samurai, who for centuries had guarded jealously their right to bear arms, found the sharing of this privilege with the lower classes as hard a blow to their pride and morale as the loss of their traditional pensions was to their livelihood. Yamagata, however, saw it as a gain rather than a loss, even in samurai terms. To him it was not a question of the old aristocracy being reduced to the level of the peasantry, but of the peasant being raised to the dignity of the samurai. Thenceforward every citizen would be expected to meet the rigorous standards and fulfill the high ideals of the old warrior caste.[15]

Yamagata also raised the period a soldier was required to serve in the reserves to

With the Meiji Restoration and Japan's increase in military power, the situation began to change. In 1876 Japan staged a show of naval might designed to intimidate the Koreans just as the Americans had intimidated the Japanese two decades before. The Japanese forced the king of Korea to sign a "treaty of friendship" according to which Korea would allow Japan special trading privileges and other rights. Not surprisingly, China protested vigorously, claiming Korea was its vassal state. Two decades of harsh words and political maneuvering followed in which both Japan and China sent troops into Korea and moved increasingly closer to armed confrontation. Eventually, the Japanese opened hostilities by firing on Chinese gunboats in July 1894.

After the issuing of formal war declarations in August, the conflict with China became known as the Sino-Japanese War.

Japan immediately showed its superior military strength and leadership. In one stunning victory after another, the new modern Japanese army and navy easily defeated the poorly organized and ill-trained Chinese forces. Chinese resistance was so weak and inept, Yamagata arrogantly but accurately remarked, that "Japanese officers did not encounter any serious problems worthy of careful consideration."[17] By the end of September, Japan had taken complete control of the Yellow Sea, the strategic body of water lying between Korea and the Chinese mainland. Japan's foreign minister, Mutsu Munemitsu, expressed in his diary the general feeling among the Japanese that victory was assured:

> The people, who before the news of . . . the [triumph in the] Yellow Sea were privately very anxious about

Japanese forces, holding high their flag, overwhelm the poorly armed Chinese in the opening of the first Sino-Japanese War. This initial battle took place as the Japanese crossed the Yalu River, the boundary separating China from northern Korea.

Representatives of the Chinese government sue the triumphant Japanese for peace. Although the treaty terms the Japanese demanded were humiliating, the Chinese had no choice but to accept them.

the final outcome, now have no doubt of an early victory. It is only a question of time before the flag of the rising sun advances to the doors of Peking [China's main city]. The spirit of the country soars to heights of ecstasy. Everywhere the people are overflowing with pride and arrogance, and intoxicated with songs and cries of victory.[18]

In the following months, the Japanese found no reason to alter this elated spirit. In October Yamagata moved his army into Manchuria, and in November the Japanese seized the Liaotung Peninsula (in southern Manchuria) and its important port city of Port Arthur. With the Japanese now in a position to march inland and attack Peking, the Chinese sued for peace. On April 17, 1895, the two nations offi-

cially ended the war by signing the Treaty of Simonoseki, which clearly favored Japan. China was forced to give up any claims on Korea, to cede to Japan the Liaotung Peninsula and the large island of Formosa (now Taiwan, located about six-hundred miles southwest of Japan) and to pay the Japanese a large cash sum. Japan's swift and overwhelming victory demonstrated to the world that a military and political power to be reckoned with had entered the global diplomatic scene.

From Elation to Humiliation

But Japan's new reputation came at a price. The Western powers, especially Russia, which also had designs on Manchuria, were concerned about the Japanese upsetting the balance of power in East Asia. On April 23, 1895, only a week after Japan's triumph, Russia, France, and Germany ganged up in what is often called the "triple intervention." They informed the Japanese that it would be wise to return Liaotung to China. And in separate communications, Russia made it known in so many words that it was willing to back up this demand with force if necessary. On May 5 the Japanese government, realizing that it was not yet ready to begin a larger conflict, backed down. For the Japanese people, the pride and elation of winning had suddenly given way to the humiliation of once more submitting to Western intimidation.

Adding to Japanese bitterness, the Russians soon pressed their own advantage in China. In 1898 the Chinese gave Russia permission to occupy part of Liaotung and

A Spectacle Rare in History

In 1908 Japanese leader Okuma Shigenobu (1838–1922) traced his country's rapid growth during the Meiji period. This excerpt from his book Fifty Years of New Japan, *quoted in* Sources of Japanese Tradition, *acknowledges Western contributions to Japanese progress.*

"By comparing the Japan of fifty years ago with the Japan of today, it will be seen that she has gained considerably in the extent of her territory, as well as in her population, which now numbers nearly fifty million. Her government has become constitutional not only in name, but in fact, and her national education has attained to a high degree of excellence. . . . Her general progress, during the short space of half a century, has been so sudden and swift that it presents a spectacle rare in the history of the world. This leap forward is the result of the stimulus which the country received on coming into contact with the civilization of Europe and America, and may well, in its broad sense, be regarded as a boon conferred by foreign intercourse [dealings with foreigners]. Foreign intercourse it was that animated the national consciousness of our people, who under the feudal system lived localized and disunited, and foreign intercourse it is that has enabled Japan to stand up as a world power. We possess today a powerful army and navy, but it was after western models that we laid their foundations by establishing a system of conscription in pursuance of the principle 'all our sons are soldiers,' by promoting military education, and by encouraging the manufacture of arms and the art of ship building."

the Russians promptly built a naval base at Port Arthur. China also allowed Russia to build a railroad line across Manchuria to Port Arthur. In the wake of these developments, Japanese public opinion favoring the use of force to expel Russia from Manchuria steadily increased. It was no secret to anyone why Manchuria was a prize so coveted by both the Russians and Japanese. For the Russians, this strategic territory represented a convenient corridor to the Pacific Ocean, where they could expand their naval power in the East by utilizing warm-water ports such as Port Arthur. For the Japanese, Manchuria was a valuable source of grain and natural resources. About Manchuria, W. Scott Morton writes:

> Geographically the region consists of a great and fertile plain, in which large-scale land development was begun only in modern times at the hands of Chinese farmer immigrants, mainly from [China's] Shantung Province. This plain produces the staple grain of the north, millet, and soybeans, legumes of high nutrient and vitamin value used also in the manufacture of paint and many other industrial products. The plain is surrounded on the east by virgin forests. . . . It has valuable deposits of gold, iron, soft coal, and other minerals. . . . Both the situation [nearby location] and the undeveloped resources of Manchuria, therefore, made it a most desirable area for exploitation by the Japanese.[19]

Such exploitation was clearly impossible, however, unless Japan could push the Russians out of the area. But Japan's leaders realized that a confrontation with this powerful nation would be far more difficult and dangerous than the fight with China had been. So they continued with their military buildup. They increased the size of the army and built factories in Japan to produce the most modern, quick-firing rifles. They also significantly increased naval strength, adding four modern battleships, sixteen cruisers, twenty-three destroyers, and more than six hundred smaller craft to the war fleet.

A Thirst for Culture and Knowledge

Not all Japan's patriotic energies and talents went into expanding the military and modernizing the country, however. The Japanese had a long and rich historical legacy of fine art, literature, drama, and leisure activities, but in the early Meiji period many Japanese had turned away from traditional culture. No longer isolated from the rest of the world, they had embraced and experimented with various aspects of Western art, music, and literature. Eventually, however, the continuing political rivalry with the West made Western culture seem increasingly less attractive to the Japanese. In the late 1800s it became a kind of fashionable patriotic gesture to reject Western arts and ideas. This trend was one important motivating factor in an overall rediscovery of traditional Japanese cultural endeavors in the later Meiji years. According to W. G. Beasley:

> In 1881, for example, a society was formed to revive interest in Japan's own traditions of painting and fine art, as distinct from those more recently

Commodore Perry and other U.S. representatives are among the spectators at this 1854 sumo *wrestling match. By 1900,* sumo *was one of Japan's most popular sports.*

brought in from Europe. [Oligarch] Iwakura [Tomomi], with some of his friends, sponsored performances of the classical No drama [formal plays in which the actors wore masks] and helped to raise the funds to build it a new theater in Tokyo's Shiba Park . . . while the following decade saw a modest renewal of interest in such minor arts as flower arrangement and the tea ceremony, often under the patronage [financial support] of newly-rich merchants and industrialists. . . . Such men also became patrons of Japanese-style wrestling (*sumo*), which by 1900 rivalled [Western-style] baseball as a national sport. Other sports of Tokugawa times, like fencing, were kept alive by the armed forces and the police.[20]

Although traditional poetry and other literature remained popular, the Japanese developed an almost fanatical interest in a more modern literary form—the daily newspaper. In the days when Japan was an isolated, closed society, no newspapers existed. But after the first daily paper, the *Yokohama Mainichi Shimbun*, appeared in 1870, the public, eager to know what was happening around the world as well as in Japan, demanded more. Dozens of new papers started up each year, and by 1890 the country had more than five hundred daily, weekly, and monthly newspapers. The government also took a keen interest in the news media. The nation's leaders discovered that a widely read newspaper could be a potent tool for educating the

Natsume Soseki (1867–1916) is now acknowledged as the greatest Japanese novelist of the Meiji period. In this excerpt (quoted in Modern Japanese Literature, *edited by Donald Keene) from his popular 1906 novel* Botchan, *the title character recalls a youthful mistake.*

"From childhood I have suffered because of the reckless nature I inherited from my parents. When I was in elementary school I jumped out of the second story of the school building and lost the use of my legs for a week. Some people might ask why I did such a thing. I had no very profound reason. I was looking out of the second-floor window of the new schoolhouse when one of my classmates said as a joke that, for all my boasting, he bet I could not jump to the ground. He called me a coward. When the janitor carried me home on his back, my father looked at me sternly and said he did not think much of anyone who dislocated his back just by jumping from the second floor. I said next time I would show him I could do it without getting hurt."

public about government policies and programs. To a degree, then, the government used the media to gain public support and build up patriotic fervor against the country's Western rivals.

The Confrontation with Russia

Russia became the continuing target of such anti-Western feelings in Japan after the Russian intrusion into Manchuria in 1898. Japanese leaders knew, therefore, that they could count on strong public support for any move that might intimidate Russia. In 1902 they made just such a move. As historian Milton W. Meyer explains:

To advance their interests in Korea, and to contain Russia, the Japanese negotiated a treaty with the British. . . . Fearful that Japan might ally itself with Russia against their own interests, the British concluded . . . the Anglo-Japanese Alliance. . . . Its terms confirmed the integrity of China and of Korea, although Britain recognized special Japanese interests in Korea. The two signatories [parties] affirmed neutrality [pledged not to get involved] in the event that one of them was engaged in war with a third party.[21]

Having vastly increased their military strength, and with the British seemingly in their corner, the Japanese now felt ready to confront the Russians. In 1903 Japan and Russia began talks concerning Korea and Manchuria. During these tense negotiations, Russia's leader, Czar Nicholas II, unwisely inflamed Japanese tempers by sending troops into eastern Russia and Manchuria. Seeing this move as a clear threat to their own security, the wary and angry Japanese broke off negotiations in early February 1904.

A few days later, on February 8, the Japanese launched a surprise night attack, striking a massive blow to the Russian fleet anchored at Port Arthur. Having blockaded the surviving Russian ships in the harbor, Japan sent forces from Korea into Manchuria and besieged Port Arthur's landward side. The town fell in January 1905, and Russian forces retreated northward along Russia's Manchurian railway line. After several small land skirmishes,

Russian artillery, seen here in action at the Battle of Mukden, could not defeat the well-organized and amply supplied Japanese war machine.

Russian czar Nicholas II. His arrogant and unfounded belief that his own forces were superior to those of Japan helped inflame the confrontation between the two nations.

the main bodies of the Japanese and Russian armies met at Mukden in southern Manchuria in a two-week-long battle. The carnage was horrendous and the casualties heavy on both sides. But thanks to the Russian army's poor leadership and inadequate supply lines, the Japanese emerged victorious in March 1905.

The Japanese had similar success at sea in May 1905. According to W. Scott Morton:

> The Russians had dispatched their Baltic fleet to reinforce the squadron at Vladivostok [a Russian port northeast of Korea]. Britain refused to allow the fleet to use the Suez Canal or any British ports en route. The Russian admiral had to round the Cape of Good Hope [in southern Africa] and refuel

at French ports in Madagascar and Indo-China [now Vietnam]. [Japan's] Admiral Togo Heihachiro guessed, correctly as it turned out, that the Russians would take the shorter route inside the Japanese islands, and he lay in wait with a powerful battle fleet in the Tsushima Straits between Korea and Japan. He achieved surprise and executed the tactic known as "crossing the T," namely steaming in column across the enemy line of advance, which enabled him to fire successive broadsides [artillery barrages], while the rear ships of the enemy, blocked by their own vessels in front, could not bring their guns to bear. Torpedo boats then went in to administer the *coup de grace* [death blow].[22]

The Russian fleet suffered a catastrophic defeat, losing thirty-two of its thirty-five ships. Russia had no more immediate military resources to call upon, so the war was effectively over.

The End of an Era

The official end of the conflict known to the world as the Russo-Japanese War came in August 1905 with the Treaty of Portsmouth. In a peace conference in the American town of Portsmouth, New Hampshire, arranged and presided over by President Theodore Roosevelt, the Japanese made a number of demands. They wanted recognition of their supremacy in Korea, as well as control of Russia's Manchurian railway and its interests in Liaotung. Japan also demanded the southern half of Sakhalin Island, located north of Hokkaido, control over which had long been disputed by the two countries. The Russians agreed to all these demands.

Japan had won many concessions from Russia, but the consequences of the war extended far beyond the bargaining table. The Japanese victory had stunned the world. By soundly defeating one of the Western powers, Japan had notified the others that its military might and political ambitions should not be taken lightly. It had resolutely set out to make itself the dominant East Asian power and had done so in less than two decades. With China and Russia defeated, Japan's power in the area was so great that when Japanese forces annexed Korea outright in 1910, no

U.S. president Theodore Roosevelt poses with Russian and Japanese representatives during the 1905 Treaty of Portsmouth negotiations held in New Hampshire.

The Old Asiatic Unity

In his 1903 work Ideals of the East, *Japanese writer Okakura Tenshin discussed the idea of destiny—Asia's destiny to be united under one guiding force, and Japan's destiny to be that very force. These excerpts are quoted in* The Emergence of Imperial Japan, *edited by Marlene J. Mayo.*

"Asia is one. The Himalayas divide, only to accentuate [emphasize], two mighty civilizations, the Chinese with its communism [group orientation] of Confucius [the ancient philosopher] and the Indian with its individualism of the Vedas [religious teachings]. But not even the snowy barriers [of the mountains] can interrupt for one moment that broad expanse of love for the Ultimate and Universal [heavenly force that sees them as the same and united]."

"The [Sino-Japanese] War, which revealed our supremacy in the eastern waters, and which as yet draws us closer than ever in mutual friendship, was a natural outgrowth of the new [Japanese] national vigor, which has been working to express itself for a century and a half. It has also been foreseen in all its bearings by the remarkable insight of the older statesmen of the period, and arouses us now to the grand problems and responsibilities which await us as the new Asiatic Power. Not only to return to our own past ideals, but also to feel and revivify the dormant life of the old Asiatic unity, becomes our mission."

Eastern or Western nation raised an objection. Perhaps it was fitting that the conclusion of this first phase of Japanese empire building coincided with the end of the Meiji era. The emperor bearing that name died in 1912, bringing the first dramatic episode in Japan's adventure as a modern nation to a symbolic close.

Chapter

3 From Admiration to Apprehension: Stepping onto the World Stage

In the two decades following the defeat of both China and Russia, Japan proved to the rest of the world that it was indeed a powerful and modern country. Japanese leaders showed that they were just as capable as their Western counterparts of playing the game of power and influence on the world political stage. In 1914, World War I broke out in Europe. With the Western powers preoccupied by that conflict, Japan seized the opportunity to expand its influence in East Asia. European and American leaders now began to worry about Japan and what it might do next. Where once the West had admired the Japanese for their rapid modernization, it now saw them as a possible threat to the stability of East Asia, an area still largely controlled by Western nations. Thus, in the 1920s these nations took steps to curb Japanese power and expansion. Such opposition deepened the resentments the Japanese already held for the West and thereby helped to lay the foundations for the next world war, in which the Japanese would seek their revenge.

French troops take up a position near the Marne River in northeastern France during World War I. Kept occupied by this great conflict, the Western powers did not devote much attention to Japanese expansion in East Asia.

Japan's Asian Lifeline

The advent of World War I gave Japan the chance to launch its second phase of empire building. When Britain, France, and other European countries lined up against Germany in 1914, the Japanese saw a golden opportunity. The Germans were distracted thousands of miles away, and the time seemed ripe for Japan to grab Emperor Wilhelm's holdings in East Asia. As a first step, the Japanese declared war on Germany. Next, they occupied territories in China's Shantung Province, which the Chinese had earlier leased to the Germans. Japan also took over German-controlled islands in the northern Pacific—the Marianas, the Carolines, and the Marshalls. As Japanese leaders had expected, the Germans were too busy with the European war to offer significant resistance.

Emboldened by this success, the Japanese quickly moved to expand their other interests in China, especially in Manchuria. In January 1915, they presented the Chinese with what became known as the Twenty-One Demands, a so-called treaty that was no more than an outright bully tactic. For example, Japan demanded the right to expand its control over the German holdings in Shantung, as well as over parts of Manchuria and Inner Mongolia, the area located east of Manchuria. According to Robert L. Worden:

> Japan also sought joint ownership of a major mining and metallurgical complex in central China, prohibitions on China's ceding or leasing any coastal areas to a third power, and miscellaneous other political, economic, and military controls, which if achieved, would have reduced China to a Japanese protectorate [a territory completely dependent on Japan].[23]

Widespread protest in China and international condemnation led the Japanese to withdraw some of the demands. But when the treaty was signed in May 1915, Japan acquired much of what it had sought.

Japanese designs on Manchuria and other Asian areas were not new. But Japan now offered a fresh justification for its takeover of these areas. Some conservative Japanese leaders, intellectuals, and writers began pushing the idea of Asian unity, and the catchphrase "Asia for the Asians" became popular. In May 1915, at the time Japan was achieving success with its Chinese demands, military strongman Yamagata summarized this idea in a private conversation with a colleague, saying:

> Manchuria is Japan's life-line. Thus, we must secure for our people the guarantee that they can settle there and pursue their occupations in peace. If this problem cannot be disposed of by diplomatic means, then we have no other alternative but to resort to arms. . . . In their essence Sino-Japanese relations are extremely simple and clear. . . . Are not Japan and China the only true states in Asia? In short, we must attempt the solution of our myriad [many] problems on the premise of "Asia for the Asians." However, Japan is an island country . . . which cannot hope to support within its island confines any further increase in population. Thus, she has no alternative but to expand into Manchuria or elsewhere. That is, as Asians, the

The Road of Progress

In 1916 Japanese university professor and political writer Yoshino Sakuzo (1878–1933) explained why Japan should move toward democracy, or constitutional government, as he put it in his article "On the Meaning of Constitutional Government." (This excerpt appears in Sources of Japanese Tradition.*)*

"Whether or not constitutional government will work well is partly a question of its structure and procedures, but it is also very much a question of the general level of the people's knowledge and virtue. Only where the level is rather mature can a constitutional government be set up. . . . However, since the trend toward constitutional government is world wide and can no longer be resisted, advanced thinkers must make the attempt to establish it firmly. They should voluntarily assume the responsibility of instructing the people so as to train them in its workings without delay. If they do not, constitutional government can never function perfectly however complete it may be in form. Therefore, the fundamental prerequisite [prior condition needed] for perfecting constitutional government, especially in politically backward nations, is the cultivation of knowledge and virtue among the generality of the people. This is not a task which can be accomplished in a day.

Think of the situation in our own country. We instituted constitutional government before the people were prepared for it. As a result there have been many failures. . . . Still, it is impossible to reverse course . . . so there is nothing for us to do but cheerfully take the road of reform and progress. Consequently, it is extremely important not to rely upon politicians alone, but to make use of the cooperative efforts of educators, religious leaders, and thinkers in all areas of society."

Japanese must of necessity live in Asia. . . . While the expansion of Japan into Manchuria may be a move for her own betterment . . . it would also be a necessary move for the self-protection of Asians and for the . . . co-prosperity of China and Japan.[24]

Trade, Prosperity, and Social Change

To the delight of the Japanese, their brazen landgrabs during World War I were largely successful and increased the size of their growing empire. Far from opposing this expansion, the Western powers officially condoned it. In 1917 the United States, France, and Britain in effect accepted Japan as a fellow imperialistic power by openly recognizing Japanese territorial gains in China and the Pacific. Recognition and acceptance of Japan as a world power was further demonstrated at the war's end. In 1919 at the Versailles Peace Conference, where the victors met to decide the fate of defeated Germany, Japan was one of the "Big Five" nations, along with Britain, France, Russia, and the United States. The Treaty of Versailles officially transferred German rights in Shantung Province to Japan. The agreement also put the stamp of approval on Japan's earlier seizures of the German Pacific island chains.

Even more impressive than Japan's World War I political gains were its economic gains in the war years. These gains signaled the country's rise as one of the world's industrial and trading giants. As W. Scott Morton explains, the Japanese

made immense strides in the building and operating of a great merchant fleet, having, in fact, become one of the world's great [freight] carriers through the heavy shipping losses experienced by Britain, Germany, and the United States in submarine warfare. The Japanese had been able in their new [ship] construction to take advantage of the newest technical advances. They . . . moved directly [from early primitive engines] to steam turbines and then to diesel engines. During World War I Japanese merchant marine income had multiplied ten times. Japan had captured a large

Delegates from many countries meet at the Versailles Peace Conference in 1919. Japan was among the "Big Five" nations, which confirmed its growing world power status.

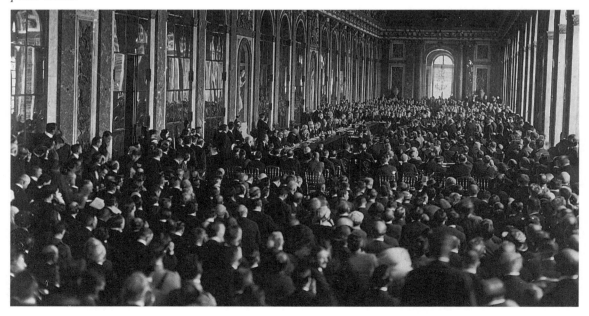

This view of a Tokyo street in 1919 reveals that the Japanese possessed modern architectural styles, trolley cars, and communications lines comparable to those of the developed Western nations.

share of the world textile trade, and had ended the war as a creditor nation with gold reserves which had increased sixfold in six years.[25]

During World War I and the postwar years, Japan's rapidly growing economy brought it domestic prosperity, and the incomes of Japanese citizens from many walks of life rose significantly. A rise in general living standards in turn stimulated social changes. After suffering disfavor in Japan in the late Meiji period, Western cultural ideas and pastimes once more came into vogue, and many Japanese enjoyed Western classical and jazz music, books, motion pictures, and sports such as golf and skiing. An increase in the number of business firms expanded the demand for secretaries and office workers. Many of these positions were taken by women, most of whom had never before worked outside their homes, or fields in the case of peasants. The general position of women, traditionally one of complete subservience to men, also changed somewhat. While before most Japanese men had treated women virtually as property, some now allowed their wives and sisters a measure of independence and a voice in family affairs. A few husbands went so far as to treat their wives as equals, something at the time still rare even in Western societies. Any such equality was strictly on the personal level, however, for legally women retained a decidedly unequal status. They could not vote, inherit or own property, choose their husbands, or receive custody of their children in a divorce.

Not surprisingly, changing social customs in the rural areas, where many poor

Some of the many Japanese women who took jobs in factories during World War I.

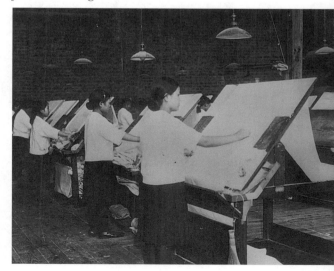

This 1923 photo captures some of the widespread devastation produced by the great Tokyo earthquake.

farmers still worked the land in a traditional manner, were slower to take effect. By far the most significant social changes occurred in the cities, which were the natural focus of economic growth and physical modernization. By chance, nature's fury played a key role in speeding up these processes in Japan's most populous region. "The great Kanto earthquake and fire of September 1, 1923," says Edwin Reischauer,

> helped accelerate the rate of social change. The great cataclysm [disaster], which destroyed half of Tokyo and

most of Yokohama and took some 130,000 lives, helped sweep away old ways and cleared the ground literally for new cities and figuratively for a new society. Downtown Tokyo became a city of wide thoroughfares [avenues] and of many great steel and reinforced concrete buildings, resembling in sections the cities of Europe and America more than those of Asia. The Marunouchi district around the main Tokyo railway station became the pride of the nation and a symbol of the new modernized Japan. Other cities followed Tokyo's lead, and soon modern office buildings of steel, school buildings of concrete, large movie houses, an occasional great stadium, and sprawling railway stations became the typical architecture of Japanese cities.[26]

Democratic Pros and Cons

Paralleling the rapid social changes of the postwar years were calls for political change, particularly a popular movement

Just one year later, in 1924, a massive rebuilding effort had already transformed most of the ruins into an impressive new modern city.

A Call for Peace

This excerpt from a speech (quoted in Sources of Japanese Tradition*) by business executive Yamamuro Sobun (1880–1950) illustrates the view held by a minority of Japanese in the 1920s, namely, that the country should coexist in peace with other nations rather than choose the path of expansion and militarism.*

"Japan can keep itself a going concern only by means of international cooperation. Under this policy . . . we can get along by producing goods of the highest possible quality at the lowest possible price, thereby expanding our foreign markets to the greatest [extent] possible. A country as deficient in natural resources as Japan buys raw materials from foreign countries at low prices and processes [these materials] at a low cost. Of course, circumstances peculiar to Japan have [modified] our development. For example, silk has been an important item. However, in addition to encouraging the expansion of this industry we must endeavor through a policy of international cooperation to establish our country as an international industrial producer of international commodities. To that end we must do our best to create an amicable [friendly] atmosphere in international relations. If we have the reputation of liking war or of being militarists, [a policy of] international cooperation will be impossible. We must resolutely follow a policy of peace. It is essential to make all foreigners feel that the Japanese have been converted from their old religion [of expansionism] and have become advocates of peace."

for a more democratic and representative government. One factor that strengthened this movement was education. Thanks to the Meiji reforms in the preceding decades, the general Japanese citizenry had become more educated, more knowledgeable about the outside world, and therefore more aware of how the democratic process worked in other countries. Also, the Japanese had become the world's most enthusiastic newspaper subscribers and readers. Editorials in the newspapers regularly criticized the government and called for political reforms, and this media stance encouraged many members of the public to do the same.

As a result, the restrictive franchise in which only a tiny minority of the population could vote became increasingly unpopular. In 1919 and 1920 the matter came to a head in the form of mass public protests in many cities. "Calls were raised for universal suffrage [voting rights]," comments Robert L. Worden:

Students, university professors, and journalists, bolstered by labor unions and inspired by a variety of democratic, socialist, communist, anarchist, and other western schools of thought, mounted large but orderly public demonstrations in favor of universal male suffrage.[27]

Many of the demonstrators sang the "Universal Suffrage Song," including the refrains:

> All this talk about "labor" being "sacred"!
> *Yoi, yoi,*
> Why don't they give us the right to vote?
> *Yoi, yoi,* democracy!
> Who harvests the rice? Who tills the fields?
> *Yoi, yoi,*
> Why don't they give us the right to vote?
> *Yoi, yoi,* democracy!
> Shouldn't everything be governed by public opinion?
> *Yoi, yoi,*
> Why don't they give us the right to vote?
> *Yoi, yoi,* democracy!
> Only by our digging coal can the machines run.
> *Yoi, yoi,*
> Why don't they give us the right to vote?
> *Yoi, yoi,* democracy![28]

In time, such protests persuaded the government to liberalize voting laws, and in 1925 full male suffrage regardless of wealth or tax status became the law of the land. More than fourteen million Japanese now could vote. Also, in the mid-to-late 1920s the two-party political system familiar in Britain, the United States, and other Western democracies became strong in Japan. The few surviving *genro* of the Meiji era exercised diminishing authority, and Diet members, both elected and hereditary, held much of the real political power.

Despite these and a few other gains in representative government, however, democracy did not take firm hold in

In 1925, leading members of the Insei-to, *a major political party, celebrate after their victory in the first election held under universal suffrage.*

Japan. There were a number of reasons for this. First, the Diet's House of Peers, with its older, more conservative members, remained the stronger of the two legislative houses and tended to make decisions in the name of the emperor. Since the constitution, at least in theory, gave the emperor several authoritarian and very undemocratic powers, the Peers constituted a roadblock to democracy. Also, whereas Britain and the United States had long-standing traditions of democratic ideals, no such framework existed in Japan. Instead, people were used to the idea of a harmonious society in which everyone pledged unswerving loyalty to the state, symbolized in the person of the emperor. Says Edwin Reischauer:

> The Meiji leaders who had come to power by championing the right of the emperor to rule, had created and fostered this tradition. . . . By building up an elaborate state cult . . . centered on the person of the emperor . . . and by indoctrinating school children with fanatical devotion to the emperor and blind faith in all statements said to represent his will, they secured for themselves the unquestioning loyalty and obedience of the people.[29]

In the face of this kind of blind loyalty to central authority, democratic leaders found it difficult both to operate and to spread their ideals.

Factors Impeding Japanese Expansion

Another reason for the continuing weakness of democracy in Japan was opposition from staunchly anti-Western militarists and nationalists. These ultra conservatives, army and navy officers prominent in their ranks, believed that adopting a Western style of democracy would make Japan weak and corrupt. They held that it was Japan's destiny to go forth, to conquer, and to rule other lands, all in the name of the emperor and the greater good of the Japanese people. By claiming that they, not the constitutional government, represented the emperor's true will, they maintained a devoted following. So these entrenched elites were able to get away with saying and doing many things that flew in the face of democratic procedure and law. Reischauer offers this summary:

> Acts of aggression abroad and, at home, acts of civil disobedience, political murders, and open mutiny were all justified as being in accord with the true will of the emperor, whose views, it was claimed, were misrepresented by the corrupt politicians.[30]

As proof that democracy did not work, the militarists pointed to the weak foreign policy record of the elected leaders. Most Japanese backed the militarists' ideal of vigorous expansion in East Asia, but throughout the 1920s the government was unable to implement this goal. One factor that impeded expansion was the rise of Chinese nationalism. Many Chinese had become tired of having their country treated as a backward area ripe for imperialist picking. Antiforeign, especially anti-Japanese, riots became increasingly frequent in the 1920s, as did large-scale boycotts of Japanese merchants and products. And the Chinese Nationalists, a group headed by political and military leader Chiang Kai-Shek, became increasingly suc-

Chinese nationalist leader Chiang Kai-Shek, whose tireless efforts to unify China posed a threat to Japanese interests in that country.

cessful in unifying and strengthening the country. These trends threatened Japanese interests in Manchuria and other parts of China and made further Japanese gains in the area difficult.

Another factor that interfered with Japanese imperialism in the 1920s was Japan's old nemesis, Russia, which now possessed a new status. After the revolution of 1917, a communist government came to power in Russia, which thereafter was known as the Soviet Union. The communists opposed Japanese expansion in East Asia because it posed an obvious threat to Soviet borders and also competed with Soviet influence in the area.

The Soviets did everything they could to hinder the Japanese, including helping to instigate a communist party in Japan in 1922. The Japanese communists boldly demanded the abolition of the emperor as a national symbol, withdrawal of Japanese troops from China, Korea, and Sakhalin Island, and recognition of the Soviet Union. Although the Japanese government tried to suppress the communist party, the group remained active and caused significant political unrest.

Still another reason for Japan's failure to expand its empire, and the factor that would have the most lasting and ominous impact, was opposition from the West, particularly the United States. By the early 1920s, admiration of Japan for its determination and boldness had given way to apprehension about Japanese expansion, which the Western powers decided to curb. In late 1921 and early 1922, nine nations, including the United States, Britain, France, Italy, China, and Japan, met in Washington, D.C., to discuss East Asian and Pacific affairs. For the Japanese, this so-called Washington Conference was another encounter with Western intimidation. Japan had no choice but to accept a number of proposals agreed on by the other nations, the most bothersome of which concerned naval power, an important key to Japanese expansion. According to historian Rinn-Sup Shinn:

Where the naval armaments race was concerned, Britain, France, Italy, Japan, and the United States—the five major naval powers of the time— agreed to limit battleship and aircraft carrier tonnage of the five nations to a ratio of five each for Britain and the United States, three for Japan, and

Delegates meet at the 1922 Washington Conference to discuss East Asian affairs. Once more, the Japanese felt intimidated and insulted by Western demands.

1.75 for France and Italy. Japan reluctantly agreed to the lower ratio when Britain and the United States pledged not to expand their bases and fortifications in the Pacific other than their existing naval installations. Nevertheless the upshot of the Washington Conference was a growing dissatisfaction in Japan with the western powers in general and the United States in particular. These powers were viewed by many Japanese as bent on [their own Western version of] military expansion and on containing Japan's influence in China.[31]

All through the 1920s a majority of Japanese saw the results of the Washington Conference both as unfair and as a humiliating loss of face to the Western powers. This diplomatic defeat, coupled with the government's failure to pursue a strong expansionist policy for other reasons, weakened the image of the representative government. At the same time these reverses played directly into the militarists' hands. Japan's most conservative elements would eventually marshal their forces, first against liberal leaders and institutions within the country, and then, with ever-deepening contempt, against the West.

Chapter

4 Asia for the Asians: The Rise of the Japanese Militarists

The weakness of Japan's civilian representative government in the 1920s helped many right-wing, ultranationalist, and militaristic groups to increase in membership and in popularity. These organizations, many of them led by conservative army officers, appealed to old Japanese values of patriotism. Their hallmark was unswerving devotion to the emperor, and their major goal was Japanese expansion and supremacy in East Asia. By the 1930s, the civilian government was unable to counter the influence of these militarists, who eventually managed to take effective control of the country and its affairs. Beginning with a campaign of naked aggression in China, they set out to build an Asian empire. Supposedly, this policy was for the good of all Asians, whom, the militarists insisted, Japan was destined to lead. Using slogans such as the old "Asia for the Asians," the militarists sought to exclude Western influences from Japan. They also became increasingly hostile toward the

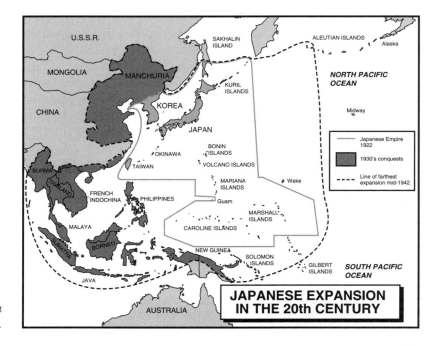

This map of the east Asian sphere in the early decades of the twentieth century shows many of the areas seized by Japan, including Manchuria and numerous island chains.

United States, which, because it openly opposed Japanese aggressions, came to represent the main obstacle to Japan's success.

Support for a Patriotic Vision

The establishment and growth of right-wing, militarist organizations in Japan in the 1920s was not a sudden or unusual development. In many ways it was a natural outgrowth of the social and political trends of the preceding half century. In the late 1800s, for example, the Meiji oligarchs had strongly stressed patriotism in the form of nearly blind obedience to the emperor and the state. And the main thrust of Japanese foreign policy from the early Meiji years onward had been expan-

Japan Takes the Third Door

Hashimoto Kingoro was a prominent right-wing Japanese militarist who tried in his writings to justify Japanese expansion into East Asia. Typical was this excerpt from his work titled Addresses to Young Men *(quoted in* Sources of Japanese Tradition*), written in 1939.*

"There are only three ways left to Japan to escape from the pressure of surplus population. We are like a great crowd of people packed into a small and narrow room, and there are only three doors through which we might escape, namely emigration, advance into world markets, and expansion of territory. The first door, emigration, has been barred to us by the anti-Japanese immigration policies of other countries. The second door, advance into world markets, is being pushed shut by tariff barriers and the abrogation [abolition] of treaties. What should Japan do when two of the three doors have been closed against her? It is quite natural that Japan should rush upon the last remaining door. . . . At the time of the Manchurian incident [1931–1932], the entire world joined in criticism of Japan. They said that Japan was an untrustworthy nation. . . . But the military action taken by Japan was not in the least a selfish one. . . . The [Western] Powers are still discussing whether or not to recognize this new nation [Manchukuo], but regardless of whether or not other nations recognize her, the Manchurian empire has already been established, and now, seven years after its creation, the empire is further consolidating its foundations with the aid of its friend, Japan."

sion in East Asia, usually by forceful military means. Generations of Japanese had grown up believing it was their country's destiny to be the number-one Asian power. It is hardly surprising, then, that the patriotic vision of a strong, militaristic Japan remained popular among a majority of Japanese citizens.

Conservative Japanese felt that the nation's largely peace-loving democrats were weakening and corrupting this patriotic vision. The civilian government consistently failed to press for expansion in Asia in the 1920s and seemed too interested in maintaining good relations with the West. It was not that most Japanese were against the Diet and representative government. They strongly desired certain democratic institutions and practices, as evidenced by

Hashumoto Kingoro, one of the leaders of the Kokuryukai, or Black Dragon Society, a right-wing ultranationalist group.

their mass demonstrations for voting rights. But they also wanted the government's policies and actions to reflect their views, which largely favored expansion.

Thus, because the militarists spoke for so many everyday citizens, large numbers of Japanese sympathized with or at least condoned the right-wing groups that grew increasingly stronger. Among the largest and most successful of these groups was the *Dai Nippon Kokusuikai*, or Greater Japan National Essence Society, which by 1919 had more than a million members. Other similar nationalist organizations included the *Kokuhonsha*, or National Foundation Society, the *Sakurakai*, or Cherry Society, and the *Kokuryukai*, or Black Dragon Society. All these groups grew larger in the 1920s by advocating a fascist-style government and society. Fascism is a right-wing, antidemocratic political system in which a single party uses dictatorial powers to control society and implement strongly nationalist policies. To these nationalist groups, a dictatorship of the emperor and the military seemed the best way to implement Japan's "destiny" of controlling Asia.

The nationalist societies were influenced by the ideas and writings of thinker Kita Ikki, who became known as the intellectual father of Japanese fascism. In his highly influential 1919 book *A Plan for the Reorganization of Japan*, he called for the elimination of the Diet and a coup d'état, or military takeover, of the civilian government, stating:

A *coup d'etat* should be looked upon as a direct manifestation of the authority of the nation; that is, of the will of society. The progressive [democratic] leaders have all arisen from popular groups. . . . In the reorganization of Japan there must be a manifestation of the power inherent in a coalition of the people and sovereign [emperor]. The reason why the Diet must be dissolved is that the nobility and wealthy upon whom it depends are incapable of standing with the emperor and the people in the cause of reorganization. . . . The reason martial [military] law must be proclaimed is because it is essential for the freedom of the nation that there be no restraint in suppressing the opposition which will come from [the nobility and the wealthy]. . . . The fundamental doctrine of the emperor as representative of the people and as pillar of the nation must be made clear.[32]

The Military Plays Its Hand

By the end of the 1920s, the right-wing societies had become so strong and so popular that some of their members felt not only justified but bold enough to begin implementing some of Kita Ikki's extreme goals. At first, the chief method was assassination, usually of a liberal politician. For example, on November 14, 1930, Prime Minister Yuko Hamaguchi was shot by a young militarist. As Milton W. Meyer explains, such random attacks, which the ultraconservatives called "heroic," were not yet part of an organized militarist plan:

> Those young military men who espoused Japanese fascism often turned to acts of heroism to promote their cause. Such a young man was termed a *soshi*, one who dedicated himself to the nation. . . . The heroes of the right performed self-sacrificial, dramatic acts and [thereby] offered themselves to the nation. . . . They possessed no precisely outlined program of action, nor did any blueprints exist on how to put an end to parliamentary government other than to assassinate persons unfriendly to the cause.[33]

The older, higher ranking military men were not yet ready to play their hand, how-

Prime Minister Yuko Hamaguchi in 1930, shortly before being assassinated by a fanatical young right-wing militarist.

Units of the Japanese Kwantung army march through southern Manchuria in 1931. The Kwantung soon began acting on its own, often without even informing the civilian government in Japan.

ever, as emphasized during an attempted coup d'état against the government in March 1931. Members of the Cherry Society, mostly low-ranking army officers, planned to attack the Diet and impose martial law. But the plot failed when senior military officers refrained from joining the coup.

It was only a matter of months, however, before higher ranking military right-wingers began to assert themselves. The leaders of the Japanese army in southern Manchuria, the Kwantung (or Guandong), became particularly bold. In September 1931, the Kwantung attacked and captured the city of Mukden, along with a Chinese force of ten thousand soldiers. Kwantung leaders claimed they were retaliating against an act of sabotage by Chinese bandits on the Japanese-controlled Manchurian railway. The actual damage, independent observers later showed, amounted to the destruction of a mere thirty-one inches of track.

The most ominous aspect of the Kwantung's action was its accomplishment without the permission or even the knowledge of the civilian government in Tokyo. The Kwantung continued boldly to act on its own, launching a rampage through the remainder of Manchuria. Japanese soldiers routinely burned villages, murdered helpless Chinese children and military prisoners, and raped Chinese women, effectively completing their Manchurian conquest by January 1932. One Japanese government official later stated that the bureaucrats in Tokyo "had no way of learning what the plans and

A group of Japanese soldiers cart off booty robbed from Chinese villagers during the Chinese-Japanese conflict of the early 1930s.

activities of the Kwantung Army were."[34] Helpless to stop its own military machine, the civilian government had no choice but to go along with the Kwantung when army leaders announced that Manchuria had become the Chinese state of Manchukuo on March 9, 1932. In fact, Manchukuo was a Japanese puppet state in which Chinese officials did the bidding of the Japanese officers who had appointed them.

One important reason for the inability of Japanese civilian leaders to stop the aggression in Manchuria, and for their after-the-fact approval of it, was lack of popular support. According to Edwin Reischauer:

> The [Japanese] people as a whole accepted this act of unauthorized and certainly unjustified warfare with whole-hearted admiration. Many businessmen and bureaucrats . . . happily accepted this expansion of the national domain and attempted to justify the acts of the military before a critical world public. The Japanese government, in fact, steadfastly maintained the fiction that there had been no war and called the whole conquest of Manchuria simply the "Manchurian incident."[35]

Typical of the many examples of domestic support for the army's actions was the widespread popularity of the "Song of the Human Bomb." This morbid tune celebrated the acts of three Japanese soldiers who destroyed a barbed wire barrier by blasting it with bombs attached to their bodies.

Japan's Divine Mission?

The trouble in Manchuria was just the beginning round of the militarists' barrage against East Asia. Widespread support at home was the first of two factors that served to encourage these men and their aggressive designs. The second factor was the relatively mild reaction of the Western powers. Not long after the creation of Manchukuo, the League of Nations, a precursor of the United Nations, investigated the situation. Its report, published in October 1932, condemned Japan as the aggressor, but the international organization took no punitive action. In fact, League officials proposed a settlement virtually recognizing Japan's "special interests" in Manchuria, in effect condoning the concept of Japanese expansionism.

The United States, which did not belong to the League, issued a stronger condemnation of Japan's actions in China. In 1932 U.S. secretary of state Henry L. Stimson announced what became known

U.S. secretary of state Henry L. Stimson angered the Japanese by forcefully stating American support for China's territorial sovereignty.

An Early Warning

A few American and other Western diplomats early recognized the dangerous course being plotted by Japan's militarists. In December 1934 the U.S. ambassador to Japan, Joseph Grew, wrote this warning (quoted from Grew's 1944 book Ten Years in Japan) *to his boss Cordell Hull, the secretary of state.*

"It would be helpful if those who [do not take the Japanese threat seriously] could hear and read some of the things that are constantly being said and written in Japan, to the effect that Japan's destiny is to subjugate and rule the world, and could realize the expansionist ambitions which lie not far from the surface in the minds of certain elements in the Army and Navy, the patriotic societies, and the intense nationalists throughout the country. Their aim is to obtain trade control and eventually predominant influence in China, the Philippines, the Straits Settlements [now Singapore and nearby islands], Siam [now Thailand], and the Dutch East Indies [now Indonesia] . . . and Vladivostok [a strategic Russian Pacific port], one step at a time, as in Korea and Manchuria, pausing intermittently to consolidate and then continuing as soon as the intervening obstacles can be overcome by diplomacy or force. With such dreams of empire cherished by so many . . . we would be [foolish] if we were to trust to the security of treaty restraints [agreed to by the Japanese] or international comity [courtesy] to safeguard our own interests, or, indeed our own property."

as the Stimson Doctrine. Among other things, the U.S. diplomat said that his country did not "intend to recognize any treaty or agreement . . . which may impair . . . the sovereignty, the independence, or the territorial and administrative integrity of the Republic of China."[36] The thrust of the U.S. position was that it would not recognize the validity of Manchukuo and would continue to help the Chinese Nationalists maintain their sovereignty. To this end, the U.S. government soon began extending loans and selling warplanes to the Chinese. This implied declaration of opposition initiated a deterioration of U.S.-Japanese relations that would grow more serious and ominous in the succeeding years.

But for the moment, the U.S. failure to take more concrete action against Japanese aggresions served to embolden Japan's militarists. They increased the frequency and threatening tone of their warlike statements, making it clear to Western nations and

Japanese democrats alike that Manchukuo represented merely a first step toward the fulfillment of Japan's "destiny." The militarists stopped short of saying openly that Japan had a divine mission to rule the world. But a number of their statements indicated that global domination might be their ultimate goal. And this goal would be partly achieved through what they termed *Kodo*, or "Way of the Emperor," a mysterious divine quality that, according to proponents, only the Japanese people and their imperial leader possessed. An arrogant statement made in 1933 by Japan's war minister Gen. Sadao Araki is typical of this attitude:

> It is a veritable measure of Providence [will of the gods] that the Manchurian trouble has arisen. It is an alarm bell for the awakening of the Japanese people. If the nation is rekindled with the same great spirit in which the country was founded, the time will come when all the nations of the world will look up to our *Kodo*. Every impediment to it [must] be brushed aside—even by the sword.[37]

Bloodbath and Suppression

The militarists eventually acted on the threat of violence within their own country, aiming their wrath at the few remaining democratic and liberal forces that opposed them. Historian Louis L. Snyder tells what happened:

> Again the approved weapon was assassination. The killers had no personal animosity against their victims, who, after all, were Japanese. But the fanatics believed that they were ridding the sacred Emperor of nefarious [evil] influences and so performing the sacred function of clearing the way for Japan's glorious future. It was too bad, they said, but [their opponents] had to go. The killers would show their personal sorrow by burning incense beside the dead bodies.[38]

A series of vicious and pitiless political assassinations in the early 1930s culminated in a 1936 bloodbath that firmly established the militarists' supremacy in the government. On February 20, fourteen hundred young military officers seized central Tokyo and murdered several liberal figures. The prime minister, Keisuke Okada, narrowly escaped death when the assassins mistook his brother-in-law for him. Former prime minister Makoto Saito and education inspector-general Watanabe were among those who were not so fortunate. The U.S. ambassador to Japan, Joseph Grew, described in his diary the heroism of Saito's and Watanabe's wives, whom the American knew well:

> It is only when such things occur in one's midst and when violent death and heroic action take place among one's friends and almost at one's door that the shock really comes home and remains. Gradually, from the accounts of friends, we can now reconstruct the way the assassinations took place, and . . . the stories . . . show the true stuff of Japanese womanhood—how [Mrs.] Saito placed herself in front of her husband [and] said, "Kill me instead; my husband cannot be spared by the country," and actually put her hand on the mouth of the machine gun until her wounds forced her aside, and how Mrs.

One indication of the growing power of the militarists was this 1934 review of military trainees staged in front of the imperial palace in Tokyo.

Watanabe lay down with her husband in her arms so that the assassins had to force the gun underneath her body.[39]

The liberals spared in this bloody purge did not dare speak out against the militarists, who thereafter either assumed government posts themselves or controlled the votes of Diet members and other civilian leaders. Fulfilling Kita Ikki's dream, Japan had become a fascist state. The militarists wasted no time in openly directing the country's foreign policy. In November 1936 they signed the Anti-Comintern Pact with Germany, which by then also had a fascist government. This agreement was designed both to demonstrate friendship between two nations with similar ideologies and to show solidarity against the Soviet Union and international communism, as represented by the Comintern, an umbrella group of communist parties from all over the world.

Meanwhile, the Japanese militarists also took a hard line on the home front.

According to Edwin Reischauer, they labeled all things not to their liking as "un-Japanese" and suppressed them.

Western ballroom dancing was severely condemned and . . . dance halls were sometimes closed. Golf and other luxury sports were frowned on. An effort was made to stop the use of English scientific and technical words in conversation and writing, while street and railway signs, which had once been bilingual, were remade with the English omitted. Students in the men's higher schools and universities, which had been noted for their independence of thought, were forced into the same patterns of rote memorizing as pupils in lower schools; participation by women in the intellectual life of the nation was discouraged; labor unions were deprived of all influence; freedom of expression in newspapers and journals was curbed . . . and a rather successful attempt was made to have the people replace rational thought on political and social problems with the use of semi-mystic phrases, such as "national crisis," "Japanese spirit," and "national structure."[40]

Unexpected Resistance

Next, the militarists turned their attention once more to China. On July 7, 1937, they attacked a town near Peking, initiating the second Sino-Japanese War. The conflict quickly escalated and by October 1938 Japanese forces had overrun the cities of Nanking, Canton, and Hankow. As in the

This 1937 photo shows Japanese soldiers rushing through an opening in a wall of a Chinese stronghold in Nanking.

1931 Manchurian invasion, the Japanese soldiers were allowed to indulge in torture, rape, and wholesale looting. But while the new Japanese aggression was brutal and in many ways effective, unexpected and fierce local resistance prevented it from taking full control of China. As W. Scott Morton puts it, the invaders

> could bomb but could not penetrate with ground forces the mountain provinces of the southwest in sufficient strength to force a decision; but they overran the main part of the country, holding all the principal cities and lines of communication. For Japan as well as China it was a costly war. Chinese guerilla forces . . . constantly attacked and overcame small isolated garrisons [military posts] of Japanese, disrupted [weapons and supply] transport, and succeeded in supplying themselves with trucks, arms, ammunition, and even uniforms from the small enemy units they had defeated.[41]

Since the fighting raged on intermittently, the Japanese were not able to gain a clear-cut victory, and the China war eventually merged with the greater conflict of World War II, which was soon to erupt.

During the initial assault on China in 1937–1938, the Japanese militarists defended their actions by citing the old idea that it was Japan's destiny to control and to lead Asia. They soon began promoting the concept of the "Greater East Asia Co-prosperity Sphere." The "sphere" was supposed to be a peaceful, prosperous Asian region, an "Asia for Asians" free from Western influences, which the Japanese would eventually create and oversee.

But the West, in particular the United States, did not buy this rationale for Japanese

Wishing for Some Action

Hino Ashihei, an official Japanese military correspondent assigned to chronicle the activities of the Japanese troops in China in the second Sino-Japanese War, penned the popular Earth and Soldiers *in 1938. This excerpt, quoted from* Modern Japanese Literature, *reveals that the soldiers stationed far from the frontlines often longed for the excitement and glory associated with military action.*

"Again today, there is the blue sky and the blue water. And here I am writing this while lying on the upper deck of the same boat [that I've been on for a long time]. I wish this were being written at the front, but [unfortunately it is] not yet. All I can tell you is about the soldiers, lolling [lounging] about the boat, the pine groves and the winding, peaceful line of the Japanese coast [which it is our job to guard]. What will be our fate? Nobody knows. The speculation about our point of disembarkation [leaving the boat] is still going on. Rumors that we are bound for Manchukuo are gaining strength. Besides, there is a well-founded report that on the Shanghai front, where there has been a stalemate [between Japanese and Chinese forces], our troops attacked and fought a ferocious battle. The story is that two days ago they advanced in force and rolled back the [enemy] line for several miles, taking two important Chinese cities. They say that big lantern parades are swirling through the streets of Tokyo, in celebration. So the war is over! And we are to be returned, like the victorious troops: That would be funny, in our case, but anyway, we are to be sent home soon! Of course, this is nonsense, some absolutely ridiculous story. Yet we cannot avoid listening when someone talks in this vein. We cannot believe it and yet we do not wish to convince ourselves that it is not true."

aggression. U.S. leaders worried that Japan's expanding empire would eventually threaten American and other Western territories and interests in the East Asian and Pacific regions. Accordingly, the United States took increasingly stronger steps to curb Japanese expansion. In 1938, for instance, the U.S. War Department pressured American manufacturers to halt sales of airplanes to Japan. And in 1940 the country banned exports to Japan of oil, steel, and scrap iron, strategic materials the Japanese badly needed to support their military efforts. East-West tensions increased further when the Japanese signed the Tripartite Pact with Germany and Italy that same year. This agreement, which created the fascist Berlin-Tokyo-

Japanese fascists celebrate the 1940 Tripartite Pact with Germany and Italy.

Rome "Axis," was designed to redivide the future world into spheres controlled by the three partners. It was also, at least from the Japanese point of view, a specific attempt to intimidate the United States.

A Secret and Fateful Decision

But the United States was not intimidated. During American-Japanese talks in 1941, U.S. officials insisted that Japan pull all its troops out of Manchuria and other parts of China. By that time, the oil embargo was hurting the Japanese and the furious militarists began seriously discussing the use of force against the United States. Secret war preparations escalated in late October 1941 when army minister Tojo Hideki, nicknamed "the Razor," became Japan's strongest and most influential leader. Tojo was a fanatical militarist and a ruthless, humorless individual who passionately hated the United States. In his view, for Japan to

fulfill its destiny, it must eliminate its number-one obstacle—the United States.

To that end, in November 1941 Japanese military leaders made a secret and fateful decision. They ordered a massive fleet of seventy-two warships to steam eastward across the Pacific Ocean toward Pearl Harbor, Hawaii, where almost the entire U.S. Pacific fleet lay anchored. Loaded with hundreds of planes and thousands of tons of bombs, the Japanese ships moved silently toward a bloody encounter that Tojo and his colleagues hoped would decisively seal the fate of the United States. In this moment of supreme arrogance and boldness, the militarists did not foresee that the fate they had sealed was their own.

General Tojo Hideki, also known as "the Razor," hated the United States and fanatically promoted anti-Western ideas and attitudes.

Chapter

5 Empire of the Sun: All-Out War in the Pacific

In an effort to cripple permanently the war-making ability of the United States, the Japanese attacked the U.S. naval base at Pearl Harbor, on the Hawaiian island of Oahu, on December 7, 1941. The United States responded by declaring war on Japan, and a series of counter war declarations followed immediately, worldwide. Within days, Japan and its Axis partners, Germany and Italy, were at war with the United States, Britain, and much of Europe, polarizing the combatants into two camps—the Axis and the Allies. (Germany had initiated hostilities in Europe in 1939 and had begun bombing England in 1940.) The titanic struggle that followed, the ordeal of total war known as World War II, also had two major "theaters," or overall regions, of military operations. In the European theater, the Allies faced off against Germany and Italy, while in the Pacific theater Japan was their solitary foe.

At first, a string of spectacular Japanese successes created the impression that the sons of the rising sun were unstoppable and invincible. In a series of lightning raids and expeditions, Japan greatly expanded its East Asian–Pacific empire. The Japanese "octopus," as many in the Allied camp referred to Japan's military, stretched out its tentacles over southern Asia, the East Indies and the Philippines,

and many Pacific island chains. Australia and New Zealand, the great Pacific bastions of Western culture, appeared to be Japan's next targets. In the wake of these unsettling events, the United States and the other Allies were unprepared to fight a major war so far from their homelands. For many months they could do little but watch helplessly as the formidable Japanese war machine ran unchecked through the Pacific.

A Rain of Bombs

In both strategy and execution, the attack on Pearl Harbor recalled the surprise assault the Japanese had launched on the Russians at Port Arthur decades before. On Sunday morning, December 7, 1941, all but three of the U.S. Navy's biggest warships were anchored at Oahu. Lining the docks of Pearl Harbor's Battleship Row were huge armored vessels, among them the USS *Arizona*, the *West Virginia*, the *California*, and the *Oklahoma*. Along with military barracks and maintenance facilities, Oahu was also home to more than four hundred U.S. bombers and fighter planes, which were parked on nearby airfields. The Americans, like the Russians before them, had badly

Basking in Reflected Glory

The first year of Japan's entry into World War II, Japan's "great year," in which its empire expanded in spectacular fashion, was made possible in large degree by the contributions of the country's industrial and business concerns. In this excerpt from Japan's War Economy, *T. A. Bisson explains the link between the factories and the battlefield wins.*

"Inauguration of the Tojo Cabinet on October 18, 1941 ushered in Japan's great year, marked by a series of far-flung territorial seizures and notable military victories. . . . This was also the great year for Japan's business circles. They reveled in a virtually unrestricted process of rounding out their cartels [huge companies that absorb smaller ones] in industry, finance and trade, while the military and naval leaders were carving out a new empire in the southern [Asian] regions. . . . For a time, the business circles were able to bask in a reflected glory, since theirs had been the economic achievements which produced the Zeros [Japanese fighter planes] that swept the skies and the bombers that humbled Anglo-American naval pride off Malaya and at Pearl Harbor. But for the business leaders . . . the close of this first year began to cast longer shadows. Already the cry for more ships and planes, that later rose to a frenzied appeal, was becoming more insistent. . . . [But for the moment] the business interests had no reason to feel unduly alarmed. . . . The first year of the Tojo regime witnessed the complete fulfillment of the monopolists' [cartel leaders'] desire to streamline the cartellization of [creation of a few large companies within] Japan's economy with the backing of state authority."

underestimated the strength and boldness of the Japanese. Assuming they would receive plenty of advance notice if the country went to war with Japan, U.S. military personnel on Oahu were totally unprepared for the massive air assault that struck them that morning.

At about 7:53 A.M., Mitsuo Fuchida, the commander of the Japanese attack planes, arrived to scout the target from a high altitude. When he saw the American ships lined up unprotected in Battleship Row, he was overcome with joy. Excitedly he radioed his pilots the code words *"Tora! Tora! Tora!"* ("Tiger! Tiger! Tiger!"), the signal that complete surprise had been achieved and the attack should proceed as planned. Seventeen minutes later, Fuchida watched with glee as 189 warplanes from the Japanese carriers *Kaga, Hiryu,* and *Akagi* roared into view.

The attackers immediately zoomed in on the U.S. base and began raining bombs on the unprotected ships and planes. Typical of the lethal bombing runs was that of young Lieutenant Matsumura from the *Hiryu*. According to historian John Toland:

> He went down to less than 100 feet and started a run on one of the ships in the outside row—it was the *West Virginia*. Usually the pilot alone released the torpedo, but today, to make doubly sure, most navigator-bombadiers were also pushing their release buttons. "*Yoi* (ready)," he called. . . . Then: "*Te!* (fire!)." As the torpedo was launched, he pulled the [control] stick back sharply. "Is the torpedo running straight?" he called to the navigator. He was afraid it

The horrendous damage done to the U.S. naval base at Pearl Harbor on December 7, 1941, is evident in this photo of burning and capsized American warships.

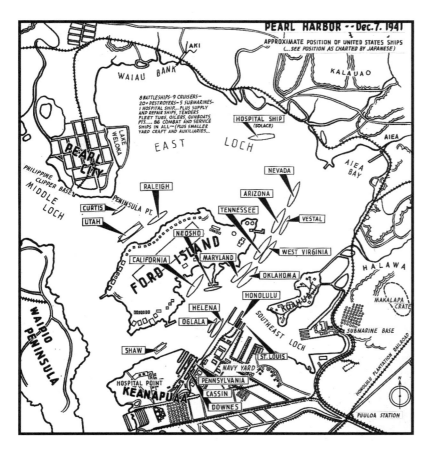

This map shows the approximate positions of the American warships anchored at Pearl Harbor on the morning they were attacked by waves of Japanese planes.

might dig into the mud. Matsumura pushed in the throttle, but instead of making the standard left turn, climbed to the right. He kept looking back to keep his torpedo in view. In the oily water he saw American sailors; they seemed to be crawling in glue. He banked further and saw a column of water geyser [spray up] from the *West Virginia*. This one moment was worth all the hard months of training.[42]

By 8:30 A.M. the attackers, out of bombs and ammunition, departed. But they were followed half an hour later by a second wave of Japanese planes, some 175 in all. By the time this second wave turned away to-ward the waiting Japanese fleet, Pearl Harbor and the neighboring airfields were smoldering ruins. The *West Virginia*, hit by Matsumura's and others' bombs, was a mass of flames, its captain and many crewmen dead. The entire front section of the *Arizona* had broken off and more than a thousand of its crew had perished. The *Oklahoma*, the *California*, and many other vessels had sustained severe damage, and 308 U.S. planes had been destroyed or put out of action. In all, 2,343 Americans died in the attack, 1,272 were wounded, and another thousand were missing. By contrast, the Japanese lost only 29 planes.

The capsized USS Oklahoma *and USS* Maryland *spew columns of black smoke shortly after the Japanese attack.*

Britain's Prince of Wales *(left) and* Repulse *were both destroyed on December 9, 1941, when waves of Japanese bombers attacked them.*

Two Great Vessels Meet Their End

This stunning victory, which had in a mere two hours all but wiped out American naval power in the Pacific, was but the opening maneuver in an overall Japanese offensive. For months, the militarists in Tokyo had been laying their plans for expansion into many Asian and Pacific regions. They clearly stated their goals for these unmistakable aggressions in the *Basic Plan for the Establishment of the Greater East Asia Coprosperity Sphere.* This secret document stated in part:

> Aggressive American and British influences in East Asia shall be driven out of the area of Indo-China [now Vietnam] and the South Seas, and this area shall be brought into our defense sphere. The war with Britain and America shall be prosecuted for that purpose. The Russian aggressive influence in East Asia will be driven out. . . . For this purpose, a war with the Soviets is expected. . . . Next the independence of Australia, India, etc. shall gradually be brought about. For this purpose, a recurrence of war with Britain and her allies is expected.[43]

To move effectively toward these far-reaching goals, Japanese leaders decided that the best strategy was to strike hard and quickly on all fronts. Therefore, within a few days of the devastating Pearl Harbor assault, the Japanese struck at the British colonies of Singapore, Malaya, Burma, and Hong Kong, in Southeast Asia. Simultaneously, Japanese troops moved into Siam and other regions of southern Asia. And as Japanese planes bombed U.S. airfields in the Philippine Islands, Japanese forces captured American-owned Pacific islands, including Guam and Wake.

Britain was even more surprised than the United States by these attacks. After all, the British had years before signed an alliance with the Japanese and had aided Japan during the Russo-Japanese War by closing the Suez Canal to Russian warships. But to Japanese leaders the necessities of the present outweighed the niceties of the past. Britain, a Western colonial power, stood in Japan's path to Eastern empire and must be removed.

In particular, the powerful Royal Navy, which guarded Singapore and other British colonies in the region, represented a prime target for Japanese military planners. The huge British flagships—the 35,000-ton battleship *Prince of Wales* and the 32,000-ton cruiser *Repulse*—were at sea about 150 miles from Singapore when squadrons of Japanese planes found them on December 9, 1941. Japanese war correspondent Yukio Waku reported:

> Columns of black smoke were sighted far on the horizon. Careful reconnaissance [inspection] told us that the smoke columns were those from the enemy fleet, which included the *Prince of Wales* and the *Repulse*. . . . Our bombers caught sight of the British Far Eastern Fleet, which seemed to have noticed our attempt and started fleeing in zigzag at full speed of 30 knots under cover of the dark clouds.[44]

Once located by the Japanese bombers, the British ships, which had no air support at all, were largely defenseless. Wave after wave of attackers swooped in for the kill, dropping their deadly explosives relentlessly and accurately. British correspondent Cecil Brown, who was aboard the *Repulse*, later filed this report describing the end of two great vessels:

> That the *Repulse* was doomed was immediately apparent. The communication system announced: "Prepare to abandon ship. May God be with you!" Without undo rush we all started streaming down ladders, hurrying but not pushing. . . . It seemed so incredible that the *Repulse* could or should go down. But the *Repulse* was fast keeling over to port [the left side] and walking

ceased to be a [reliable] mode of locomotion [movement]. . . . Men were lying dead around the guns. . . . There was considerable damage all around the ship. . . . As I go over the side, the *Prince of Wales* half a mile away seems to be afire, but her guns are still firing. . . . Swimming about a mile away, lying on top of a small stool, I saw the bow of the *Wales*. . . . When [it] sank, the suction [of the water] was so great it ripped off the life belt of one officer more than 50 feet away. . . . The gentle, quiet manner in which these shell-belching [battleships] went to their last resting place without exploding was a tribute of gratitude from two fine ships for their fine sailors.[45]

The Fall of Singapore

With the protective British fleet crippled, Singapore was wide open to Japanese attack. Yet surprisingly, the assault did not come from the sea. Because the rear of the city faced seemingly impenetrable jungles, the British had built their main defenses on the seaward side. Seeing this as a tactical mistake to be exploited, the Japanese had shrewdly trained many troops in the brutal skills of jungle fighting, and these forces attacked Singapore from the land. After three days of hard fighting by both sides, the Japanese commander issued a surrender ultimatum that stated in part:

> In the spirit of chivalry [fair play] we have the honor of advising your surrender. Your army, founded on the traditional spirit of Great Britain, is

A Hollow but Respected Tradition

Ironically, though Japan was controlled by right-wing military men from 1936 to 1945, the Diet continued to meet as it had before, giving the illusion that the civilian government still possessed real authority. In their book The New Japan: Government and Politics, *Harold S. Quigley and John E. Turner explain:*

"An impressive new building to house the national legislature was dedicated in November 1936. It occupied a commanding site and was the finest modern building in Japan. If the speeches of the dedication rang somewhat hollowly at the end of that year of political assassinations, it can be said at least that the Diet met regularly throughout the war. In but one instance was the term of a House of Representatives prolonged beyond its legal expiration date—April 30, 1941—and that for one year only. However annoying the antics [routine speeches, debates, and campaigns] of the party leaders [may have been to the militarists] . . . they could not be brushed off by closing the doors of the Diet. Only the emperor could have done that, by initiating an amendment to the constitution, a line of action which neither his advisors in brass [military men] nor those in silk [civilian consultants] ventured to suggest. So [exemplifying Japanese respect for tradition] the annual sessions [of the Diet] sanctioned by the constitution, and special sessions as well, continued to the end of the war."

defending Singapore, which is completely isolated. . . . From now on resistance is futile and merely increases the danger to the million civilian inhabitants without good reason, exposing them to infliction of pain by fire and sword. . . . Furthermore, we do not feel you will increase the fame of the British Army by further resistance.[46]

The British reluctantly complied with the ultimatum and surrendered. The Japanese had lost more than 9,000 troops taking the colony but in the process had captured a British army of 130,000 men,

to crown the greatest land victory in Japanese history. The news of the fall of Singapore had an electrifying effect on the Japanese populace. Along with the defeat of the Americans at Oahu, here was further evidence that the Japanese, Asians fated to lead other Asians, could vanquish the arrogant white Westerners. Did not Japan, led by its divine emperor, have the gods' blessing in this long overdue punishment of those whose hated black ships had once intimidated the country? To celebrate, the Tokyo government distributed two bottles of beer and a package of red beans to every Japanese family. Children under thirteen received caramel drops and other candies. The surge of confidence that gripped the nation was well illustrated by a front-page headline and article in Japan's third largest newspaper, the *Asahi Shimbun:*

> GENERAL SITUATION OF PACIFIC WAR DECIDED. To seize Singapore Island in as little time as three days could only have been done by our Imperial Army. Japan is the sun that shines for world peace. Those who bathe in the sun will grow and those who resist it shall have no alternative but ruin. Both the United States and Britain should contemplate the 3,000 years of scorching Japanese history. . . . With the fall of Singapore the general situation of war has been determined. The ultimate victory will be ours.[47]

A British tank rolls through Burma in early 1942 during the brief and futile British resistance to the massive Japanese invasion.

A Relentless, Well-Coordinated Offensive

The triumphant Japanese heaped other defeats and humiliations on their Western enemies. British-controlled Burma (now Myanmar), a large region strategically located west of Siam and south of China, was an important prize for Japan for two reasons. First, it was a source of many valuable raw materials, particularly oil, timber, and rubber. Second, it was the so-called back door to China, and the Japanese saw it as a stepping-stone to complete subjugation of the Chinese. As Louis L. Snyder tells it:

> The Japanese assault on Burma was synchronized with that on Malaya [the peninsula south of Siam], but it was to take somewhat longer because the country was larger. Two days after Pearl Harbor, advance Japanese units penetrated the Burmese border. . . . The main strike came on January 15, 1942, when a powerful force of shock troops infiltrated [sneaked] through the jungles and in two weeks captured Moulmein, opposite Rangoon [Burma's main city, now Yangon]. . . . Once again Japanese mobility and proficiency in jungle fighting paid big dividends. Crossing the broad Salween River, the Japanese circled around to the north of Rangoon, while other units slipped across the Gulf of Martaban to hit the city from the south and west. On March

6, 1942, the British evacuated the great port. . . . The Japanese entered Rangoon the next day.[48]

The Philippines, a group of 7,083 islands lying south of Japan and near the coast of Southeast Asia, constituted another prime target for Japanese conquest. Wresting control of the Philippines from the United States would effectively eliminate American influence from the region. It would also give Japan free access to the rich oil and mineral deposits of Java and other Dutch islands situated west of the Philippines. On December 8, 1941, the Japanese attacked U.S. planes at Clark Field near Manila, the Philippine capital. After American air power had been almost wiped out, Japanese forces landed at several strategic points on Philippine coasts and overwhelmed unprepared American troops. The Americans and many Filipinos soon fled

Manila, after which Japanese planes bombed the city, igniting devastating fires. The U.S. commander, Gen. Douglas MacArthur, ordered his troops to retreat to the Bataan peninsula on the western end of the large island of Luzon, where Japanese forces surrounded them. Fearing that MacArthur would fall into enemy hands, a potential disaster for the American war effort, high-ranking U.S. officials evacuated the general from Bataan. After holding out as long as possible, the thousands of besieged Americans and Filipinos finally surrendered on April 9, 1942.

Some seven hundred miles to the north of Bataan, another Western stronghold, the British colony of Hong Kong in southern China, also fell to the relentless, well-coordinated Japanese offensive. John Toland explains that by Christmas Eve in 1941,

Japanese invasion forces move through a jungle area of the Philippines, an island group strategic to the conquest and control of southeastern Asia.

the Japanese held most of Hong Kong's mountainous thirty-two square miles. The British forces were split in two and their final [defensive] lines were crumpling. There was little ammunition left and only enough water for another day or so. By Christmas morning those defenders were overrun who were cut off at the narrow Stanley Peninsula on the southern end of the island, and uncontrolled groups of Japanese began butchering the wounded and raping Chinese and British nurses. The main force at Victoria, the capital of Hong Kong, was also close to being overwhelmed. . . . Major-General C. M. Maltby, military commander of the colony . . . held off until 3:15 before reluctantly ordering his commanders to surrender. It was a humiliating end to British rule in China—and even with surrender the [Japanese] atrocities [brutal and inhuman acts] continued throughout Christmas night.[49]

Resistance Futile

The harsh treatment the Japanese victors inflicted on their prisoners in Hong Kong was not an isolated incident. It was instead part of a strict overall occupation policy designed to keep conquered populations from offering resistance to Japanese rule. In each conquered area, first came a brutal act or series of acts meant to demoralize and set an example for the subjugated people. The Americans and Filipinos who surrendered at Bataan, for instance, were forced on a horrifying death march in which thousands died of exposure, physical abuse, and out-and-out murder. Then came long months and sometimes years of occupation in which Japanese commanders instituted a code of harsh and rigid rules that usually punished the slightest disobedience with death. The code in the Japanese-controlled Philippines warned:

U.S. general Douglas MacArthur led the American and Filipino forces during the Japanese assault on the Philippines. President Roosevelt ordered his evacuation, lest one of the most valuable U.S. military leaders fall into enemy hands.

Japanese War Movies

The Japanese, like their enemies in the United States and other Allied nations, immortalized their wartime victories and campaigns in propaganda films. In this excerpt from his book Films and the Second World War, *Roger Manvell comments on the expense and attention to detail lavished on many of these films.*

"The Japanese successes were celebrated in a number of notable feature films. *The War at Sea from Hawaii to Malaya* (December 1942, the anniversary of Pearl Harbor) was directed by Kajiro Yamamoto, a highly experienced filmmaker who had been working in the [Japanese film] studios since 1920. Made at exceptional cost (almost ten times the average budget for a first-line feature) it celebrated the 'spirit of the Navy which culminated in Pearl Harbor,' reconstructing in a documentary style the building up of the navy over the years to a level capable of achieving so great an assault. . . . The use of special effects and miniatures [ships, planes, buildings] was so effective that, after the war, sections filmed in this way were accepted by the American authorities as if they were real. Meanwhile, other theaters of war were featured in Tetsu Taguchi's *Generals, Staff and Soldiers* (1942), filmed in North China under strict control of the Japanese military authorities and reflecting war as experienced at every level in the army. Tadashi Imai made *The Suicide Troops of the Watchtower* (1942), an action film in the documentary style produced in cooperation with the Korean film industry, in which the Korean [anti-Japanese] guerilla resistance forces were represented as 'bandits.'"

Anyone who inflicts, or attempts to inflict, an injury upon Japanese soldiers, shall be shot to death. If the assailant, or attempted assailant, cannot be found, we will hold ten influential people who are in or about the streets of municipal cities where the event happened.[50]

Needless to say, the new order imposed by the Japanese did not bring their fellow Asians the peace and liberation promised by the creators of the Greater East Asia Coprosperity Sphere. Rather, Japan's ruthless occupation policies brought only hatred and the increasing desire to resist.

But for the moment any resistance to the Japanese octopus seemed futile. In the first six months of the Pacific conflict the Japanese had amassed a truly impressive run of victories. They had crippled the American and British Eastern fleets and captured hun-

A view of part of the terrifying Bataan "death march," in which thousands of American and Filipino prisoners perished.

dreds of thousands of Allied soldiers. Japan's already formidable empire had quickly expanded to include millions of square miles of territory, encompassing the lands between India in the west and Hawaii in the east, and between Siberia in the north and Australia in the south. In fact, the Australian continent of almost three million square miles was the next logical target for the Japanese military steamroller. Taking Australia would give Japan tremendous quantities of natural resources and room for population expansion. Australia's fall would also demoralize the Allies, who, Japan's leaders reasoned, would think twice before meddling in Japan's new Asian sphere.

But the Japanese had made a serious error in judgment. They had dangerously underestimated the logistical potential and stubborn resolve of their opponents, most especially the United States. Ambas-

sador Joseph Grew once again delivered an early prediction that would eventually prove correct. Still at his post in Tokyo on December 8, 1941, despite the opening of hostilities the day before, Grew recorded in his diary:

> Once they [the Japanese] attacked Hawaii it was certain that the American people would rise up in a solid unit of fury. Senator [Burton K.] Wheeler [of Montana] was quoted on the radio as saying that the United States must "lick hell out of the Japanese." This may be easier said than done; it may take a very long time and we may get some serious knocks before our full power is able to register. But in the long run, Japan's defeat is absolutely certain, for the American people, once aroused, won't let go.[51]

6 The Flames of Defeat: Japan Risks and Loses All

Japan's early spectacular victories in the Pacific war did not signal the ultimate defeat of the Allies, as the Japanese had so ardently hoped. Instead, the short-lived success of the Japanese *of*fensive proved to be the prelude to an even more spectacular *de*fensive as the United States, like an awakening giant, unleashed its mighty wrath upon Japan.

Clearly, the Japanese militarists never realized the huge potential of natural resources, food production, military technology, and human energy and ingenuity the United States possessed. Once mobilized, this formidable potential translated itself into a colossal outpouring of armies, weapons, and war supplies. Tens of thousands of American factories employing millions of workers operated twenty-four hours a day, seven days a week. The result was nothing short of awesome. Only one year after Japan's surprise attack on Pearl Harbor, U.S. war production equaled the entire industrial output of Japan, Germany, and Italy combined. Thus, one vital chapter in the story of Allied victory in World War II tells of how the Axis countries were buried under a seemingly unending avalanche of American war production.

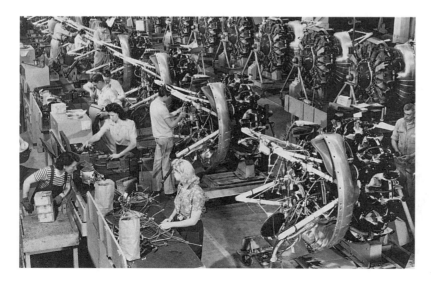

Typical of the massive U.S. war production effort was this assembly line of dive bomber engines in a Douglas Aircraft plant in 1943.

In the face of the U.S. onslaught, Japanese forces had no choice but to fall back. Less than a year after they had initiated the conflict, they began an increasingly desperate and bloody retreat westward across the ocean toward their homeland. Other humiliating defeats came in the East Asian strongholds they had recently fought so hard to wrest from the British, the Dutch, the Chinese, and the Americans. Eventually, the once mighty Japanese empire shrunk and collapsed. In its place stood its last fortress—the Japanese home islands—the inhabitants grim but still proud and defiant as the Allied forces relentlessly closed in on them.

Showdown at Midway

The first great turning point in the war, the event that transformed Japan's advance into a retreat, was the Battle of Midway. Located at the western tip of the Hawaiian Islands about eleven hundred miles from Oahu, the tiny island of Midway became the target of a major Japanese offensive in mid-1942. This surprise assault, the Japanese war planners hoped, would destroy the remainder of the U.S. fleet. It would also open the door to conquest of the Hawaiian island chain and thereby eliminate American influence from the Pacific once and for all. To these ends, Japan committed a huge naval force to the top secret Midway operation: 11 battleships, 8 aircraft carriers carrying more than 700 planes, and 21 submarines. The overall commander was the head of Japan's navy, Adm. Isoroku Yamamoto, a military genius who had suggested the Pearl Harbor attack. In

Admiral Isoroku Yamamoto, the Japanese naval leader whom the Americans viewed as their most dangerous Japanese opponent.

charge of the aircraft carrier force was Adm. Chuichi Nagumo.

With only 3 carriers and 350 planes, many of them flown by inexperienced pilots, the Americans were severely outnumbered and outgunned. But the U.S. fleet, commanded by Adm. Chester W. Nimitz, had one all-important strategic advantage. The Americans knew when and where the attack was coming. U.S. intelligence experts had recently broken the code the Japanese forces used to exchange important information, and a decoded message had revealed the date and location of the invasion.

On June 4, 1942, Yamamoto and Nagumo, unaware that the Americans were

U.S. admiral Chester W. Nimitz commanded the U.S. fleet in its stunning victory over the Japanese at Midway in 1942.

caused him to hesitate and make costly errors in judgment. Eventually, new squadrons of American fighter craft moved in for the kill. As historian Edwin P. Hoyt describes it in his book *Japan's War*, the *Akagi*, carrying Nagumo himself,

> was still turning to launch position [when] American dive bombers attacked. . . . Admiral Nagumo was caught with decks full of planes, and no fighter cover. The *Akagi* took one bomb on the flight deck amidships, and one on the port side aft. The first bomb set off the bombs [stored] in the hangar deck, and they began to blow up. The second bomb set fire to the planes loaded with torpedoes, and they began exploding. In a few minutes the fires were so bad that . . . Nagumo could escape to another ship only by going down a rope from bridge to deck, and then over to be picked up by a cruiser's boat. The story was almost the same on the carrier *Kaga*. She was hit by three

prepared, launched the offensive. At first, the operation went as the Japanese had planned. But as the morning progressed, initial and largely ineffective attacks on Nagumo's carriers by waves of U.S. planes

This photo, taken at the height of the Battle of Midway, shows Japanese planes attacking the USS Yorktown. *Japanese successes in the battle were few, however, and eventually the Japanese turned away in full retreat.*

A U.S. Marine tank unit on the Pacific island of Guadalcanal in August 1942. Fighting on this and other Japanese-held islands was heavy and bloody.

bombs and in a few minutes, that ship, too, was floating wreckage.[52]

On June 6, after more destructive bombing by U.S. planes, Admiral Yamamoto reluctantly ordered his forces to retreat. The American carriers and planes pursued them, sinking more of Yamamoto's ships. In all, the Japanese lost more than 5,000 men, 4 carriers and many other ships, and 322 planes. When the victorious Americans finally broke off the chase, the remnants of the Japanese fleet headed for a shameful homecoming. It was the first naval defeat in Japan's history.

Paid for in Blood

The unexpected defeat at Midway upset the Japanese leaders' timetable for Pacific conquest. They had to cancel temporarily their plans to invade Australia and New Zealand. They also had to go on the defensive, for the U.S. Navy, which clearly had recovered from its setback at Pearl Harbor, was now on the attack. And the British and other Allies now launched their own offensives against the Japanese octopus. The Americans assaulted the Japanese-held island of Guadalcanal, located northeast of Australia, in August 1942. After taking the island, U.S. forces moved on to the nearby Russell Islands and then to the Solomon island chain. Meanwhile, the Australians, aided by the Americans, invaded and won the large island of New Guinea, north of Australia. While the British, strengthened by American arms and supplies, counterattacked all across East Asia, the United States invaded the Gilbert, Marshall, and Caroline island chains. Through 1943 and 1944, island after island, fortress after fortress fell to the Allies as they inched their way toward the Japanese homeland.

The proud Japanese soldiers did not suffer these defeats lightly. They fought valiantly, often recklessly, and made the Allied troops pay in blood for every inch of captured territory. The Japanese troops believed in their hearts that their losses were only temporary setbacks and that the Allies were the real aggressors. Japanese soldiers all around the Pacific war theater took the defiant attitude expressed by their comrades based in China, who chanted the marching song:

Taking loving care of trees and grass,
The Japanese troops march through Hunan Province.
How kind their hearts are!
Behold, the clouds there and rivers here
Appear just as they are in our home-land.
These sights impress our soldiers' manly breasts.
With worn shoes they plod onward.
Blood streams onto the soil;

Let us defend this forest and that mountain with our blood.
Our enemies are Anglo-Americans, the white-faced demons.[53]

The soldiers' "worn shoes" were a telling sign of the growing deterioration of the Japanese war effort. Military weapons and supplies became increasingly scarce as the Allies destroyed or captured supply bases and whole armies. The factories in Japan tried desperately to resupply Japan's forces. But with sources of raw materials falling into enemy hands and increased military conscription causing a shortage of trained workers at home, the task became hopeless. A number of Japanese garrisons, or military outposts, became stranded and lacked the means to fight on after the Allies cut vital supply lines.

U.S. soldiers use devastating flame throwers to smoke out Japanese troops from a blockhouse on Kwajalein, one of the Marshall Islands, in 1944.

Defeated and surrounded by Allied soldiers, many young Japanese waited in vain for reinforcements to come to their aid. One unnamed youth on a besieged Philippine island left a note that read:

> I am exhausted. We have no food. The enemy are now within 500 meters from us. My dear Mother, my dear wife and son, I am writing this letter to you by dim candlelight. Our end is near. What will be the future of Japan if this island shall fall into enemy hands? Our air force has not arrived. General Yamashita has not arrived. Hundreds of pale soldiers of Japan are awaiting our glorious end and nothing else.

In 1944, U.S. troops disembark and go ashore on Saipan, where Japanese resistance was unusually fierce.

This is a repetition of what occurred in the Solomons, New Georgia, and other islands. How well are the people of Japan prepared to fight the decisive battle with the will to win?[54]

The Supreme Sacrifice

In truth, the people, like the troops in the field, were increasingly less prepared to fight. Japanese civilians in the home islands also began to go without essentials as shortages of food and medicine became more and more common. And still the government repeatedly called on the people for sacrifice. Soon after the disastrous fall of the island of Saipan in the Marianas in June 1944, in which thousands of Japanese committed suicide rather than surrender, Tojo addressed the nation. In a speech on July 18, he said:

> Our empire has now been confronted with a situation which in all our history is the most important. It affords us, at the same time, the rare opportunity to crush the enemy and win the victory. . . . Let us all of our one hundred million people together, renew our pledge and our determination to make the supreme sacrifice and concentrate the traditional fighting spirit of our country handed down through three thousand years to the attainment of the ultimate victory, thereby setting the Mind of His Imperial Majesty at rest.[55]

Indeed, the fighting spirit of a people ingrained with nearly a thousand years of samurai warrior tradition rose to

Three Cheers for the Emperor

The ancient samurai ideals of unswerving devotion to duty and leaders, and of shame and disgrace in defeat, are captured in this last radio message of the Japanese commander at Okinawa in 1945 (quoted in Hans Dollinger's The Decline and Fall of Nazi Germany and Imperial Japan*).*

"More than two months have passed since we engaged the invaders. In complete unity and harmony with the Army, we have made every effort to crush the enemy. Despite our efforts the battle is going against us. My own troops are at a disadvantage, since all available heavy guns and four crack battalions of naval landing forces were allocated [assigned] to Army command. Also, enemy equipment is greatly superior to our own. I tender herewith my deepest apology to the Emperor for my failure to better defend the empire, the grave task with which I was entrusted. The troops under my command have fought gallantly, in the finest tradition of the Japanese Navy. Fierce bombing and bombardments may deform the mountains of Okinawa but cannot alter the loyal spirit of our men. We hope and pray for the perpetuation of the empire and gladly give our lives for that goal. To the Navy Minister and all my superior officers I tender my sincerest appreciation and gratitude for their kindness of many years. At the same time, I earnestly beg you to give thoughtful consideration to the families of my men who fall at this outpost as soldiers of the Emperor. With my officers and men I give three cheers for the Emperor and pray for the everlasting peace of the empire. Though my body decay in remote Okinawa, my spirit will persist in defense of the homeland."

the defense of the empire and homeland. All over the war zone, garrisons of Japanese soldiers, their positions hopeless, ran at Allied machine guns in wild suicidal *banzai* charges. They died by the thousands for the glory of their emperor. Many others committed *seppuku*, as the proud samurai had done in ages past, rather than surrender to the hated Americans. Typical was the gruesome death of

an admiral named Ohnishi. According to historian Rikihei Inoguchi, the admiral's aide found that

> he had disembowelled himself [slit open his abdomen] in the traditional manner with a Japanese sword. The abdominal cut was cleanly done, but the following attempt by the admiral to slit his throat was not so successful.

When the aide arrived the admiral was still conscious and said, "Do not try to help me." Thus, refusing . . . medical aid . . . he lingered in agony until six o'clock that evening.[56]

Such scenes became more common as American forces pushed ever closer to the home islands. On February 19, 1945, thirty thousand American marines attacked the tiny island of Iwo Jima, located 750 miles southeast of Japan and one of the last stepping-stones in the American advance. After nearly a month of furious and bloody combat, much of it hand-to-hand, the island fell. On March 17, the Japanese commander, General Kuribayashi, penned the following comments and orders:

> The battle is approaching its end. Since the enemy's landing, even the gods would weep at the bravery of the officers and men under my command. . . . However, my men died one by one and I regret very much that I have al-

lowed the enemy to occupy a piece of Japanese territory. Now there is no more ammunition, no more water. . . . Our garrison will make a general attack against the enemy tonight. . . . Everyone will fight to the death. No man will be concerned about his life.[57]

Most of Kuribayashi's remaining men sacrified themselves in one final desperate *banzai* charge. A few days later, the general, wounded and disgraced, faced north in the direction of the Imperial Palace and, in the manner of his proud ancestors, tore open his abdomen.

Japan a Furnace

At the time of Iwo Jima's fall, the Americans, their carriers now situated close to the home islands, had already begun massive saturation bombing raids on Japanese

U.S. Navy and Coast Guard landing craft deliver supplies to American forces on Iwo Jima during the huge 1945 U.S. offensive on the island.

The rubble in Tokyo after the massive and destructive U.S. bombing raid of March 9, 1945. Some historians maintain that such large conventional raids might have convinced the Japanese to surrender without the U.S. resorting to the use of the atomic bomb.

cities. Day after day in the early months of 1945, waves of U.S. planes dropped thousands of tons of explosives. Thousands of civilians died horribly, and the survivors escaped into the countryside to become impoverished refugees in their own land. The nightmarish rain of death seemed to reach an awful peak on the night of March 9, 1945, when a squadron of 280 U.S. planes released more than two thousand tons of incendiary, or fire-producing, bombs over Tokyo. The bombers, says Edwin Hoyt,

> came in low, at 4000 and 5000 feet, scattering their incendiaries. . . . The fires were caught by the high winds, and the heat made the winds whirl faster until a fire storm was created, swirling winds of flame leaping across streets and open places. . . . At first many householders tried to get up on their roofs and brush the incendiaries off. Many died that way, burned horribly. . . . Others tried to flee . . . but they could hardly move fast enough through the narrow streets. Often the

buildings crashed down upon them, or the fire leaped forward and cut them off. . . . Whole blocks erupted and went up [in flames] all at once and in a few minutes had collapsed into rubble, burying more hundreds of people. . . . There was virtually no fire fighting to be done in the ordinary sense. The firemen rushed here and there, trying to save people from trapped buildings, trying to guide them out of the hell that their city had become.[58]

An estimated two hundred thousand Tokyo residents died that night, many charred to ashes, their identities forever erased. And thousands more in other cities suffered similar fates. "Over the whole of Japan," says historian Mamoru Shigemitsu, who was serving as Japan's foreign minister at the time, "tens and tens of thousands were burnt to death. Day by day Japan turned into a furnace, from which the voice of a people searching for food rose in anguish."[59] Many wondered if it would not be better to admit defeat and end the terrible carnage. But the country's militarist leaders, claiming to speak for the emperor, refused to consider surrender. In the traditional samurai way, they chose instead to save face by fighting on, and if necessary by sacrificing the entire nation. "One hundred million die together!" they demanded (using an exagerrated figure), and these twisted words became the newest catchphrase among the people. "If the Emperor ordained it," remarks Shigemitsu, "they would leap into the flames. That was the people of Japan."[60]

"Man Is Only Mortal"

By April 1945, the Allies had begun to sever the last tentacles of the Japanese octopus. As the Americans attacked Okinawa, only three hundred miles south of the home islands, the Japanese braced for the "final battle." Once before, when the mighty Mongol hordes had threatened the nation, the divine *kamikaze*, the wind

from heaven, had destroyed the enemy in a last-minute miracle. In desperation, the deeply religious Japanese prayed that the gods would not abandon them in this second great national crisis.

As if in answer to that prayer, from Japan's military ranks arose a new brand of *kamikaze*—the suicide pilot. Japanese flyers had crashed their bomb-laden planes into enemy ships before. But never had such wild acts of self-annihilation been committed in an organized manner, on such a large scale. At Okinawa, for example, the *kamikazes*, some fifteen hundred strong, became an essential part of the defensive plan. These young pilots did not have to be forced to this grim duty. Indeed, proud to offer their country the ultimate sacrifice, they approached their certain deaths in a calm, resigned, and dignified manner, as shown by a *kamikaze* fighter's farewell letter to his family:

> Man is only mortal. Death, like life, is a matter of chance. Yet destiny, too, plays a part. I feel confident in my ability in tomorrow's action. Will do my

A Japanese kamikaze *plane attempts to crash-dive onto a U.S. aircraft carrier off the coast of the Marianas in 1945. Such suicide assaults caused sporadic and occasionally serious damage to U.S. ships.*

utmost to dive head-on against an enemy warship to fulfill my destiny in defense of the homeland. . . . It is my firm belief that tomorrow will be successful. It is my hope that you will share this belief.[61]

Many a young Japanese pilot went to his death exhibiting this same courage and confidence. And the damage done to the Americans was significant. Typical was the *kamikaze* attack on the U.S. carrier *Enterprise* off Okinawa on May 14, 1945. According to American eyewitness Georges Blond:

All the batteries were firing: the 5-inch guns, the 40 mm. and the 20 mm., even the rifles. The Japanese aircraft dived through a rain of steel. It had been hit in several places . . . but it came on . . . the line of its wings as straight as a sword. . . . Flaming and roaring, the fireball passed in front of [the ship's bridge] and crashed with a terrible impact just behind the forward lift. The entire vessel was shaken, some forty yards of the flight deck folded up like a banana skin. . . . The explosion killed fourteen men. . . . The mortal re-

---

A One-Way Ride

In this tract, quoted in Hans Dollinger's The Decline and Fall of Nazi Germany and Imperial Japan, *Japanese historian Rikihei Inoguchi describes a special type of Japanese* kamikaze *craft called the* Ohka.

"The *Ohka* ('cherry-blossom'), a small single-seated wooden craft, contained 1,800 kilograms of explosives. Carried to within 20,000 meters of the target by a twin-engined bomber, it would then be released to plummet towards its goal, accelerated by blasts of its five rockets. From 6,000 meters altitude it had a range of 30,000 meters. The *Ohka* pilot would ride in the mother bomber until the action area was approached. He would then climb through the bomb bay of the mother plane into the narrow cockpit of the bomb. When enemy targets had been verified and their position made known to the pilot, he would signal his readiness to the crew in the bomber; he would pull the release handle and would be on his way in this missile of destruction, only minutes from the target. Once the release handle was pulled, it became a one-way ride for the *Ohka* pilot. When this weapon became known to the Americans, they gave it the derisive [mocking] name of 'Baka' ('foolish') bomb."

The deck of the USS Bunker Hill *after the vessel suffered considerable damage in a* kamikaze *raid in 1945.*

mains of the pilot had not disappeared. . . . The entire crew marched past the corpse of the volunteer of death. . . . [His] buttons, now black, were stamped . . . with the insignia of the *kamikaze* corps: a cherry blossom with three petals.[62]

In all, the *kamikazes* killed hundreds of American sailors, sank 34 ships, and damaged 288 other vessels. But these desperate and valiant acts were ultimately in vain. Though they created great fear and havoc in the U.S. fleet, they made but a tiny dent in the unstoppable American war machine.

The Power That Drives the Sun

By the summer of 1945 that formidable machine had crippled Japan's armies, annihilated its navies, and pounded dozens of its cities to ashes. Yet still the militarists refused to admit defeat. And so the Americans unveiled the deadliest weapon in their arsenal, one that had been developed at huge expense and in great secrecy during the entire course of the war. Now this ultimate destructive device—the atomic bomb—was ready for use.

The Japanese in southern Honshu's industrial city of Hiroshima, the first atomic target selected by U.S. leaders, were in the midst of their everyday routines on the morning of August 6, 1945. At 8:05 three American B-29 aircraft appeared over the city of 340,000 people. Many enemy planes had flown over the area before, and bombers usually came in waves. Thus most people paid the B-29 trio little attention, assuming they were merely reconnaissance craft. At 8:15, one of the planes, the *Enola Gay*, let loose its four-ton atomic device, nicknamed Little Boy by the Americans, and the bomb detonated a few seconds later at an altitude of eighteen hundred feet. In a blinding flash of light, the power that drives the sun was

The first U.S. atomic bomb, nicknamed "Little Boy," one of the devices that brought Japan to its knees and in the process launched the modern nuclear age.

unleashed on Hiroshima, reducing the city to flaming rubble in less than a minute.

In the hours following the blast, those who had survived in one piece combed through the ruins and tried to help the wounded and dying. Among these heroic but largely futile attempts was that of a priest, who, according to historian John Hersey,

> got lost on a detour round a fallen tree. . . . He heard a voice ask . . . "Have you anything to drink?" He saw a uniform. Thinking there was just one soldier, he approached with . . . water. . . . He saw there were about twenty men, and they were all in exactly the same nightmarish state: their faces were wholly burned, their eyesockets hollow, the fluid from their melted eyes had run down their cheeks. . . . Their mouths were mere swollen, pus-covered wounds, which they could not bear to stretch enough to admit the [water].[63]

Tens of thousands of people died in Hiroshima that day, and many thousands perished later from injuries and the effects of atomic radiation. And still the Japanese leaders would not surrender. The Americans dropped leaflets over Japan, stating:

The devastating damage done by the Hiroshima bomb is evident in this photo snapped shortly after the world's first atomic attack.

Telephone Poles like Toothpicks

In this excerpt from his book The War: A Concise History, *historian Louis L. Snyder describes some of the physical effects of the atomic bomb that leveled Hiroshima on August 6, 1945.*

"This one bomb, holding in its vitals a destructive force of 20,000 tons of T.N.T., descended five miles [from the bomber that dropped it], exploded before it landed, and left no crater. The violent blast following the flash crushed trees and telephone poles as if they were toothpicks, ripped sheets of metal from buildings, squashed buildings, and lifted streetcars from their tracks. When the great rolling cloud of dust and smoke, spiraling upward to form a long-necked mushroom, lifted, some 60 percent of Hiroshima had vanished—about 4.1 square miles of a city of 6.9 square miles. Hiroshima had become a trash heap. Five major industrial targets were obliterated. Thousands never knew what hit them. At least 78,000 were killed outright, more than 10,000 were never found, and 37,000 were injured, without counting those who later developed serious disease from exposure to the deadly gamma rays. . . . Streets were littered with fire-blackened parts of shattered houses. Sheets of flame whipped through the city. Panicky people fled in every direction. The eyebrows of many were burned off and skin hung loosely from their faces and hands. Others, in uncontrollable pain, held their arms forward as if they were carrying something. Some vomited as they staggered along. Throughout the area of impact there was a strong odor of ionization, an electric smell given off by the bomb's fission [atom splitting]."

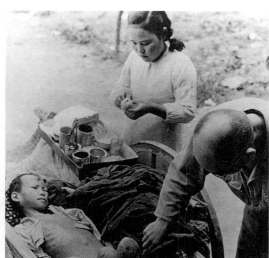

A young victim of the U.S. atomic attack on Hiroshima receives treatment.

The tell-tale mushroom cloud of the U.S. atomic device unleashed on the industrial city of Nagasaki on August 9, 1945.

America asks that you take immediate heed of what we say in this leaflet. We are in possession of the most destructive explosive ever devised by man. . . . We have just begun to use this weapon against your homeland. If you have any doubt, make inquiry as to what happened to Hiroshima. . . . We ask that you now petition the Emperor to end the war. . . . You should take steps now to cease military resistance. Otherwise, we shall resolutely employ this bomb and all our other superior weapons to promptly and forcefully end the war.[64]

Enduring the Unendurable

The forceful end the Americans had promised came after a second atomic device had obliterated Nagasaki, in Kyushu Province, on August 9, 1945. Although many of the militarists now saw that fighting on was hopeless, a few clung to their dreams of national suicide. The two groups debated the country's fate for a few more days until the emperor, Hirohito, broke the deadlock by indicating his earnest desire to see the national ordeal end.

For months the Japanese people had endured unbelievable privation and suffering. On August 15, they had to endure the ultimate humiliation—surrender. Millions stood at attention, crying openly, as Hirohito, in a radio broadcast to the nation, called for an end to the bloodshed and cruelty. Most listened enraptured, for they had never heard his voice. The only way to peace, he said sadly, is by "enduring the unendurable and suffering what is insufferable," and the people, though filled with shame and despair, silently nodded in obedience.[65]

Japan's grand dreams of empire had disintegrated in the flames of defeat. The Japanese, says Edwin Reischauer, "had risked all and lost all. Eighty years of prodigious effort and extraordinary achievement lay in ruins. For the first time in

Accepting Surrender

On August 15, 1945, Emperor Hirohito discussed acceptance of the Allied demand for Japan's surrender in this speech to his top military advisers (quoted in Edwin P. Hoyt's Japan's War*).*

"My attitude has not changed from last Friday. I have given very careful thought to the situation both of the world and Japan and come to the conclusion that we should not continue the war. True, there are certain misgivings about the preservation of the national polity [governing system]. After studying thoroughly the enemy's offer, however, I cannot but notice their good will. Everything depends, after all, on our people, whom I trust. So I am for acceptance of the [surrender] Declaration. I am resolved to do anything that is requested of me. If you think I should appeal to the nation through radio I will do so. No doubt our people, especially the soldiers, will be shocked by Our decision. If necessary I am ready to talk directly to the armed men. I wish the cabinet would start drafting the Rescript [announcement] of acceptance to the Declaration as soon as possible."

history Japan felt the tread of a foreign conqueror."[66] On September 1, 1945, ninety-two years, one month, and twenty-three days after Commodore Perry's squadron had steamed into Edo Bay, a new, vastly more powerful American fleet entered the same waters. This time the dreaded black ships had come to stay.

Chapter

7 My Enemy, My Friend: The Postwar Occupation

When the Pacific theater of World War II shut down in mid-August 1945, Japan was a devastated land. More than two million Japanese, one-third of them civilians, had died in the conflict. More than 40 percent of the total combined area of the country's cities had been reduced to ashes, and more than half of the urban dwellers either were dead or had become refugees roaming the countryside. With agriculture in decline and transportation of goods disrupted, many people lacked food and other essentials. The general feeling of despair that prevailed nearly everywhere was heightened by a mood of depression over the humiliating surrender and by fear of what the victorious American soldiers might do. Afraid that looting, murder, and rape would be widespread, many families sent their women and children into hiding.

But the American occupation of Japan was not characterized by such acts of vengeance. The object of the occupation was not to seek retribution from the Japanese but rather to help them reconstruct their country. The Americans immediately showed their earnest desire to rebuild Japan, to transform it into a responsible democratic nation, one that could and would coexist in peace with its former enemies. Many Allied leaders

expected heavy Japanese resistance to such drastic reforms. But they were proven wrong as from the ashes of their ruined cities the Japanese rose to the occasion. Humbled and eager to bury the mistakes of the past, they cooperated fully with the reorganization of their society, a transformation that went as far or farther than that of the Meiji era. The changes the country underwent in the 1945–1952 occupation period were fundamental, far reaching, and successfully implemented on all levels. As political scientist Robert Ward puts it, "The occupation was perhaps the single most exhaustively planned operation of massive and externally directed political change in world history."[67]

In the Style of a Shogun

The prelude to the American occupation of Japan was the formal surrender, signed on the USS *Missouri* in Tokyo Bay on Sunday morning, September 2, 1945. Hundreds of U.S. and Allied officers watched as a nine-member delegation, headed by Japan's foreign minister Mamoru Shigemitsu, boarded the ship. Representing the Allies, Gen. Douglas

Aboard the USS Missouri on September 2, 1945, U.S. officers look on as General MacArthur signs the documents containing Japan's formal surrender to the Allies.

MacArthur, who had less than a year before helped to liberate the Philippines from the Japanese, grasped a microphone and said:

> It is my . . . hope and indeed the hope of all mankind that from this . . . occasion a better world shall emerge out of the blood and carnage of the past—a world founded upon faith and understanding—a world dedicated to the dignity of man and the fulfillment of his most cherished wish—for freedom, tolerance and justice.[68]

Their manner grim but dignified, the Japanese then signed the surrender documents. MacArthur and other Allied representatives did the same. A few minutes later, a huge flight of more than two thousand Allied planes passed over the ship, and then over Tokyo, in a final majestic demonstration of Allied power. Japan's reluctant and uncertain encounter with foreign occupation had begun.

The Allies' first step was to set up the Allied Council for Japan in Tokyo. The council, composed of representatives from the United States, Britain, China, and the Soviet Union, was an advisory body designed to aid the Supreme Commander for the Allied Powers, or SCAP. Appointed as SCAP was General MacArthur, who held undisputed authority to approve or reject all occupational policies and actions. In effect, MacArthur was a dictator who could decide the course of Japan's future. But unlike the usual dictatorship, his rule was designed solely to carry out the main Allied objective—to rebuild Japan and transform it into a peaceful and friendly nation. MacArthur's personal manner was formal, strict, and often arrogant, which irritated many of the American and Allied officers who worked under him. But the Japanese, who were used to such qualities in their leaders, appreciated his style. W. Scott Morton explains:

> Somewhat in the style of a shogun he was [thorough and exacting] in the

performance of his duties, but in his bearing rather dignified and aloof. He turned up in his office in the modern Dainishi Insurance Building near the Emperor's palace promptly each morning in a black limousine and returned to his quarters after a hard day's work without any attempt at fraternizing [socializing] or even going about the country on inspection tours. This was precisely the conduct expected and appreciated by the Japanese. MacArthur's sense of . . . destiny seemed at times pompous and egotistical to the . . . Americans; but these very qualities, combined with his essential fairness, impressed the Japanese and gave them a needed feeling of confidence.[69]

Purging the Militarists

MacArthur's first task was to demilitarize Japan, or eliminate its war-making capabilities. This included the removal of the militarists and ultranational fanatics who had led the country to its ruin. This prime objective had first been stated in the Allied surrender demands made the preceding July, which called for an elimination

for all time [of] the authority and influence of those who have deceived and misled the people of Japan into embarking on world conquest, for we insist that a new order of peace, security and justice will be impossible until irresponsible militarism is driven from the world.[70]

In an awesome display of armed might, more than two thousand Allied planes fly over the Missouri *at the conclusion of the surrender ceremony.*

Based directly on this precedent, MacArthur's first official occupation policy, the *Basic Initial Post-Surrender Directive*, addressed the problem head-on and left no room for debate or compromise:

> Japan will be completely disarmed and demilitarized. The authority of the militarists and the influence of militarism will be totally eliminated from her political, economic, and social life. Institutions expressive of the spirit of militarism and aggression will be vigorously suppressed.[71]

MacArthur wasted no time in implementing this policy. In his first few weeks as SCAP he abolished Japan's army and navy ministries and ordered the destruction of tons of ammunition and military equip-

General MacArthur stands with Emperor Hirohito shortly after the beginning of the American occupation.

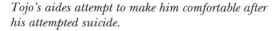

Tojo's aides attempt to make him comfortable after his attempted suicide.

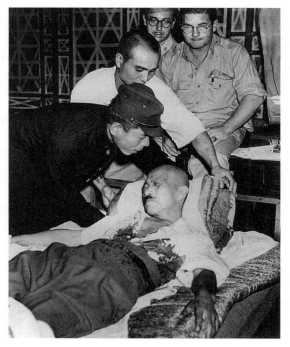

ment. At the same time, factories that had turned out weapons and ammunition immediately had to begin converting to peaceful civilian production. MacArthur and his staff also methodically rooted out and arrested the nation's top-ranking militarist leaders. Some escaped this dragnet by committing *seppuku*. Tojo, the most powerful of the group, shot himself in the chest seconds before his arrest, but American doctors saved his life. An Allied court conducted war crimes trials that sentenced Tojo and six other former leaders to death by hanging and eighteen others to life imprisonment for their roles in planning and prosecuting the war. Of some 4,200 lesser officials who were tried, about 700 were executed. And almost 190,000 former army officers, ultranationalists, and other fanatics were banned for life from serving in government posts or other influential public positions.

Because Emperor Hirohito had been only a figurehead ruler during the war, the Allies did not press charges against him. Such a step would likely have been counterproductive anyway. The Japanese people still revered Hirohito and might have reacted violently to such a move. However, MacArthur insisted that the emperor publicly renounce his status as a divine being. Complying with this order from the SCAP, on New Year's Day in 1946, Hirohito told his people that their relationship with him should no longer be based on "the false conception that the emperor is divine or that the Japanese people are superior to other races."[72] Past customs forbidding discussions about the emperor or debates about his edicts were cast aside, and people were free to talk about him like any other person.

Attacks on the Old Guard

In this excerpt from his 1949 book Prospects for Democracy in Japan *(quoted in* The Japan Reader: Postwar Japan, 1945 to the Present)*, T. A. Bisson, an expert on modern Japanese history and culture, describes the extreme public and media backlash against the militarists during the early occupation period.*

"During these early months the people responded eagerly to every forward step taken by General MacArthur. They took immediate advantage of the Civil Liberties Directive [giving the people the right of free expression]. Overnight the press and radio waves were filled with vigorous attacks on the old regime [and] the wartime leaders. . . . Six months later these sharp attacks on government policy became embarrassing to the occupation authorities, and they were gradually curbed through stricter radio control and support to old-line editors and publishers. In the fall of 1945, however, the air of Tokyo was electric with the unleashing of long pent-up emotions and suppressed resentments. . . . Popular feeling at this period was bitterly critical of the old leaders who had led Japan into the war. Freedom of speech and the press gave it every opportunity to be heard. The establishment of civil liberties, on the other hand, did not mean that the field was clear for an *equal* struggle between the old and new forces. Fifty years of indoctrination under the old regime left effects on patterns of thought and action that could not be wiped out in a few months. . . . This heritage was a fortress of the old Japan which the occupation could not take by storm."

As the American occupation began, Japanese peasants still worked large tracts of farmland in the traditional manner. Sweeping land reforms were a part of the new order imposed by the Allies.

Hope for a Better Life

In facing the truth about the emperor and themselves, the Japanese lost a romantic fantasy that had colored and defined their national character for more than two thousand years. But in severing this link with their past, in a sense they grew up as a people. They calmly and bravely accepted the emperor's admission that he was an ordinary man and in so doing, psychologically speaking, they entered the modern era. The peaceful and courageous way in which the Japanese accepted this and other drastic changes during the occupation surprised and amazed many American officials. George Atcheson, an American political adviser who reported the progress of the occupation to President Harry Truman, wrote to Truman in November 1945:

> [The Japanese are] generally in a mood for reform and change, and this is apparent from the ready man-

ner in which they have absorbed the shocks of the various political directives. Contrary to most predictions, they were not horrified to learn that they may now discuss the emperor. They were startled when the emperor called on General MacArthur [thus signifying the SCAP's superior position]; but the humiliation over that was felt chiefly by the officials. It is not going too far to say that at least the urban people are even beginning to feel some hope that they will eventually have a better life.[73]

Indeed, one large portion of the Japanese population—the millions of poor peasants who worked the land—received almost immediate benefits from occupational reforms. Before 1945 about half the country's farmers did not own their own land. Instead, conforming to practices dating from Japan's feudal past, they were tenant farmers. In exchange for a roof over their heads and enough to eat, they worked parcels of land for rich landlords who lived elsewhere. These poor tenant farmers had little or no chance for self-expression or advancement in life. For fear of losing the small portion they had, they usually did whatever their landlords told them to do, including vote a certain way (although between 1936 and 1945 militarist rule made election results largely meaningless).

The sweeping occupational land reforms begun early in 1946 both eliminated most absentee landlords and made cheap land available to millions of former tenants. At MacArthur's direction, the government purchased all land in excess of ten acres per family and sold it for reasonable prices to the poor farmers. Says Japanese scholar Fukutake Tadashi:

> This reform was practically completed within the short space of a little over two years, and as a result the area of tenanted land, which before the war had been approximately 53 percent for riceland and 40 percent for dry land, fell to below 10 percent.[74]

Millions of Japanese were thankful to the Americans for giving them what Japanese leaders had so long denied them. The former tenants now had both land of their own and the freedom to vote for whomever they chose.

The New Constitution

Because of its influence on voting rights, land reform went hand in hand with MacArthur's political reforms, in which he vigorously pushed for the democratization of Japan. His *Post-Surrender Directive* stated:

> The Japanese people shall be encouraged to develop a desire for individual liberties and a respect for fundamental human rights, particularly the freedoms of religion, assembly, speech, and the press. They shall also be encouraged to form democratic and representative organizations.[75]

The earlier Japanese experiment with democracy helped make the democratization process go relatively smoothly. First, the Japanese Diet constituted at least a basis for a democratic legislature. Although the essentially dictatorial rule of the militarists had reduced the Diet to a mere rubber stamp for their policies, in principle it was a democratic parliament. And the Japanese were already accustomed to the voting process. Most voters eagerly turned out for the first postwar election, granted by the Allied occupiers in April 1946.

But Japan was not yet a true democracy. What was missing was a real and workable democratic constitution. In October 1945, MacArthur asked a Japanese statesman named Shidehara Kijuro to serve as the country's prime minister until elections could be held and also to draft a new constitution. Kijuro was a courageous individual who had resigned from public life in the 1930s to show his opposition to the militarists. After accepting the prime ministership, he selected a cabinet agreeable to the SCAP and appointed a committee to consider the new constitution. But the Japanese, still strongly influenced by tradition, were reluctant to make significant changes in the old Meiji constitution they had known all their lives. Early in 1946 they submitted to MacArthur what amounted to a

A New Hope for Japan

On March 6, 1946, Gen. Douglas MacArthur made this announcement (quoted in The Japan Reader: Postwar Japan, 1945 to the Present, *edited by Jon Livingston et al.), informing the Japanese people that the emperor and the government had drafted a new constitution. In reality, MacArthur's staff had drafted the document and translated it into Japanese.*

"It is with a sense of deep satisfaction that I am able today to announce a decision of the emperor and the government of Japan to submit to the Japanese people a new and enlightened constitution which has my full approval. This instrument has been drafted after painstaking investigation and frequent conference between members of the Japanese government and this headquarters following my initial direction to the cabinet five months ago. Declared by its terms to be the supreme law for Japan, it places sovereignty squarely in the hands of the people. It establishes government authority with the predominant power vested in an elected legislature, as representative of the people, but with adequate check upon that power. . . . It leaves the throne [emperor] without governmental authority or state property, subject to the people's will, a symbol of the people's unity. . . . It severs for all time the shackles of feudalism and in its place raises the dignity of man under protection of the people's sovereignty. . . . Foremost of its provisions is that which, abolishing war as a sovereign right of the nation, forever renounces the threat or use of force as a means of settling disputes with any other nation. . . . The Japanese people thus turn their backs firmly upon the mysticism and unreality of the past and face instead a future of realism with a new faith and a new hope."

---

touched-up version of the Meiji document. The supreme commander startled them by rejecting their work outright.

MacArthur then ordered his own staff to write a completely new constitution. The finished product, which went into effect on May 3, 1947, guarantees civil and human rights in largely the same manner as the U.S. and British constitutions. Two articles make the Japanese version unique.

First, it recognizes the emperor, who, though now seen as mortal, remains a deeply revered symbol of the nation. "The Emperor shall be the symbol of the State and the unity of the people," the constitution proclaims, "deriving his position from the will of the people with whom reside Sovereign power."[76] This statement makes it clear that the people hold ultimate authority over the emperor instead of the

The statesman Shidehara Kijuro served as Japan's prime minister during most of the occupation years.

other way around. The other factor that makes the Japanese constitution unique is its strong renunciation of war and aggression. Article 9 states:

> Aspiring sincerely to an international peace based on justice and order, the Japanese people, forever, renounce war as a sovereign right of the nation, or the threat or use of force, as a means of settling disputes with other nations.[77]

Another article of the new constitution had an effect on Japanese society nearly as significant as that of the rejection of militarism. This was the recognition of equality between the sexes. According to Article 24, women now had the right to choose their husbands instead of being forced into marriages arranged by their fathers or brothers. Women also gained the rights to divorce their husbands and to own and inherit property. This law did not wipe away discrimination against women overnight, for many men continued to treat their wives as second-class citizens. But the new law provided a first step in a social process that over time greatly elevated the status and treatment of Japanese women.

A Peace Unparalleled in History

Japan underwent many other reforms during the postwar occupation period. Of these, one of the most significant was in education. The Americans saw that instituting long-lasting democratic and other reforms would be difficult if new generations of Japanese continued to use outmoded learning methods and materials. As Edwin Reischauer explains:

> An effort was made to . . . shift the emphasis throughout [the different school levels] from rote memory work and indoctrination [in ultranationalist thinking] to training young people to think for themselves as members of a democratic society. Textbooks were entirely revised to eliminate militaristic and nationalistic propaganda. . . . In addition, the levels beyond the initial six years of primary school were made over to conform to those customary in America: the three-year junior high school, three-year senior high school, and four-year college, or university, as it is always called in Japan. . . . The new system [widened] educational opportunities . . . and produced in time what seemed almost like a new breed of

Japanese students on their first day of primary school in the town of Himeji. Educational reforms were a key element of the Allied occupation plan.

young Japanese—more direct, casual, and undisciplined than their pre-war predecessors, but at the same time more independent, spontaneous, and lively.[78]

These educational reforms, along with many other changes the occupation forced on Japan, in a sense gave the Japanese a blueprint for a new society. Although the vast majority of citizens cooperated and eagerly implemented the changes, a few from the old guard remained wary of these Western ways. In part they resented being forced to change. But they also doubted that democracy could work as fairly as the Americans claimed it could. A few clung to the belief that President Truman, a civilian, lacked the authority to control MacArthur, whom they saw as just as big a militarist as any produced by Japan. According to this view, MacArthur would, if he chose, continue to rule Japan as a virtual dictator, proving the weakness of U.S. democracy. It came as a shock to many Japanese, therefore, when in April 1951 Truman suddenly dismissed MacArthur over a policy disagreement unre-

lated to Japan. This event taught the doubters a valuable lesson; what they learned about the strength of a democratic system was summarized by Reischauer:

For all the American preaching about democracy during the earlier occupation years, the Japanese were amazed and deeply impressed to see that a single message from the American civil government could in actuality end the authority of a great military [leader], who to them had seemed all-powerful.[79]

Not long after MacArthur's removal, the seven-year occupation of Japan ended. Believing that they had successfully rebuilt the country and set it on the path of peace and democracy, the Allies felt confident in allowing the Japanese to stand on their own. On April 28, 1952, representatives of the United States, Japan, and more than forty other nations met in San Francisco to sign a treaty officially ending the Pacific war. The document also recognized the sovereignty of the new Japan.

Changing Japanese Culture

Liberal Japanese writer and thinker Hasegawa Nyozekan held the view that Japan eventually would have become democratized on its own, even without Western influence or intervention. What the country needed was a break with former feudal cultural values, which the militarists perpetuated. He summed up this idea in this tract from his 1952 book The Lost Japan *(quoted here from* Sources of Japanese Tradition*).*

"The American [occupation] decrees issued with respect to freedom and democratization in the internal administration of Japan resulted in five major changes: the enfranchisement of Japanese women (through granting of the vote); the encouragement given to the formation of labor unions; the liberalization of school instruction; the abolition of institutions which tended to cause the people to live in fear; and the democratization of the economic structure. These five great changes in the government of the nation followed a course which the history of the modernization of Japan and of the Japanese themselves would have taken anyway if left to its natural tendency; they were, in fact, the direction towards which Japanese history was pointed. The history of Japan since the early '30s was distorted by the mistaken designs of the men in power, but the process of modernization itself was uncompromisingly carried out. We should not forget that its penetration into the very core of the Japanese nation and people made possible a political system which could serve as the external structure for Japan's emergence as a sound, strong, free, and democratic country. It became a basic condition of the culture of the race. We must, therefore, examine whether or not the culture of the Japanese people today is of a nature capable of turning Japan into a truly and completely modern nation. . . . During the Meiji Era the nation and people advanced boldly in the historical process of modernization which permitted Japan to break out of her isolation and stand among the nations of the world. When we reached the '30s, however, Japan was carried away by the tide of an age of world reaction, and there ensued a revival of feudalistic Japanese institutions. That our nation should have been plunged into destruction by . . . a union of the military and civil [authorities] proves that there had been no break in the 'feudalistic' nature of the forms of our characteristic racial, political, and social activities. . . . Thus, as a basic condition for the reconstruction of Japan as a free and democratic nation, a change in our cultural nature itself must be planned and executed."

American and other Allied diplomats watch as Shigeru Yoshida, chief Japanese delegate to the San Francisco Peace Conference, signs the peace treaty.

Shigeru Yoshida, the leading Japanese delegate, formally thanked the Allies for "a magnanimous [generous] peace unparalleled in history."

Yoshida then declared, "The Japan of today is no longer the Japan of yesterday. We will not fail your expectations of us as a new nation, dedicated to peace, democracy, and freedom."[80] These were not hollow words. By channeling into peaceful economic pursuits the same talent and enthusiasm they had put into foreign conquests, the industrious Japanese would soon far exceed the world's expectations.

Chapter

8 Economic Miracle: The Triumph of Modern Japan

On their own after signing the peace treaty with the United States and other former enemies in 1952, the Japanese continued with the reconstruction of their country begun during the occupation. Thanks to the success of occupation policies and the hard work and good will of the Japanese people, the transition was relatively smooth and uneventful. In October 1952, just five months after gaining their sovereignty, the Japanese held their first postoccupation election. In general, older conservative politicians who had worked closely with the occupation forces were elected to the highest positions. These leaders were determined to maintain the momentum of the ongoing recovery. Comments Rinn-Sup Shinn:

> The ruling elite, comprised mainly of former prewar [democratic] politicians and bureaucrats, were generally united in their efforts to bring about a rapid economic recovery and growth, to maintain a democratic political system, and to cultivate close ties with the United States as a most practical means

Japanese citizens cast their ballots in the country's first postoccupation election in 1952. Most of the winners were moderates and conservatives who had strongly supported the Allied occupation measures.

of securing benefits for Japan's economy and security.[81]

At first, the economic recovery remained steady but proceeded slowly. By the late 1950s and early 1960s, however, Japan's economy was growing far more rapidly than that of any other nation. This was due primarily to the talent and extraordinary hard work and discipline displayed by the Japanese people. The country's continued economic expansion from the early 1960s to the late 1980s, often referred to as the "economic miracle," established Japan as one of the world's commercial giants. At the same time, Japan showed itself to be a strong democracy and a friend to the United States and other former adversaries. Mutual suspicions and competitive feelings have never totally disappeared from the U.S.-Japanese relationship. But these differences are now resolved through diplomacy and the marketplace rather than on the battlefield.

Government and Industry

One of the key elements in Japan's economic success in the postwar era was the unique nature of some of its laws and political policies. Because of the Japanese constitution's renunciation of war, the country no longer channeled large portions of its financial resources into armaments and foreign military campaigns. For defense, Japan now counted mainly on the United States. After removing its occupation forces in 1952, the United States continued to maintain military bases on Okinawa and other islands and promised to defend Japan against any would-be aggressors. Freed of the need for military expenditures, the Japanese could and did invest most of their resources in revitalizing the country and expanding industry and business.

A group of Japanese businessmen and businesswomen. In the postwar world, Japan's business community became the heart of the country's productive output, in the same manner that the military had dominated the nation's output in the preceding generation.

Japan also benefited greatly from a close and largely uninterrupted partnership between government and industry. This bond was possible partly because the same major political party, one steadfastly dedicated to creating economic growth, remained popular and in power for decades. According to Robert L. Worden, in the early 1950s,

> continual fragmentation of parties and a succession of minority governments led conservative forces to merge the Liberal Party with the Japan Democratic Party . . . to form the Liberal Democratic Party (LDP) in November 1955. This party held power continuously from 1955 through [the early 1990s]. Its leadership was drawn from the elite who had seen Japan through the [Pacific war] defeat and occupation; it attracted former bureaucrats, local politicians, businessmen, journalists, and other professionals, farmers, and university graduates.[82]

The LDP regime, led by a succession of progressive prime ministers, generously supported the rebuilding of Japan's heavy industries, which had been devastated during the war. In addition to extending large loans, the government arranged special licenses from foreign countries, especially the United States. These licenses made it easy for Japanese business leaders and managers to obtain the latest technical innovations for factories, business firms, and laboratories. In 1956 the government established the Science and Technology Agency within the prime minister's office. This agency coordinated and promoted the acquisition and use of modern advanced technology by Japan's various industrial and business concerns. In time this emphasis on

Japan's name is added to the seating roster in the United Nations organization in 1956.

technology had a profound effect on Japan's economy. The factories became modern and highly efficient, and at the same time the Japanese became increasingly adept at producing technical equipment, such as electronic devices and parts.

The LDP-led government realized that to keep the economy growing, it was essential to have steady access to foreign markets for Japanese goods. So Japanese leaders tried hard to establish and maintain good trade and diplomatic relations with other nations. One important step was gaining acceptance into the United Nations organization in 1956. This helped to promote the country's image as a peace-loving, responsible member of the international community.

The Japanese put extra effort into maintaining a good, workable relationship with the United States. This was partly because of the special bond forged between the two nations during the postwar occupation, and also because America represented a vast and valuable market for Japanese goods. So for the most part, in matters of international dispute Japan backed the United States and its allies. The only serious political dispute between the Americans and Japanese occurred in 1960, when the two parties negotiated a new Treaty of Mutual Cooperation and Security. Essentially a renewal of the U.S. role as Japan's protector, the agreement provided that U.S. troops and military bases would, for the foreseeable future, stay on Japanese soil. Many Japanese felt that the American presence was a painful reminder of the past and protested the treaty. Massive street demonstrations and political unrest caused a number of Japanese cabinet members to resign. Japanese-American relations, which remained polite but somewhat cool through the 1960s, markedly improved after the U.S. gave control of the island of Okinawa back to the Japanese in 1972.

Factors in Japan's Success Story

Government support of industry and maintenance of good foreign relations were not the only factors that contributed to Japan's economic success story. A significant slowing of the country's population growth was important, as well. In the first half of the century, increasing population had been a problem for Japan because the country lacked sufficient farmland and natural resources. This, after all, had been one of the Japanese leaders' major reasons for so vigorously seeking expansion into other parts of Asia. Reaching almost eighty million in the war years, Japan's population was more than ten times more densely packed than that of the much larger United States. But in the second half of the century, says Edwin Reischauer,

> [Japan's] growth in per capita GNP [gross national product, or the country's overall economic output] was

Modern Japan's population density, more than ten times that of the United States, is dramatized in this typical view of Tokyo commuters on their way to work.

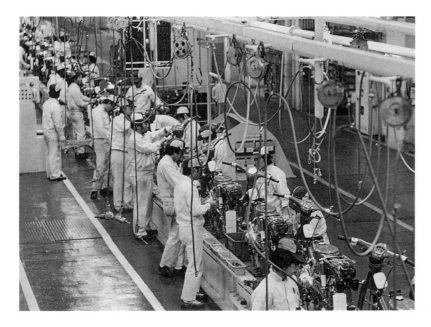

Modern, efficient assembly lines like this one in a Honda auto plant in Suzuka, Japan, contribute to the country's tremendous economic prosperity.

aided by a decided slowdown in population growth. . . . In the course of the 1950s and 1960s, the rate of births slowed down rapidly, until it produced only a little over 1 percent population growth per [year] and gave promise of stabilizing around 135 million in the year 2000. Public and private advocacy of birth control . . . and lax abortion laws, which were not enforced in any case, contributed to this decline, but the basic reason, as elsewhere in the world, was probably the rapid urbanization of Japanese society. The typical city family became limited to two children, which is usually all there is room for in a small urban apartment and all the family can afford to see through the long years of education at a university.[83]

Another factor that aided Japan's economic success was the industrious and disciplined nature of the Japanese people as a whole. After their disastrous defeat in the war, citizens at all social and economic levels felt it their duty to help put the country back on its feet. Journalists Leonard Silk and Tom Kono described this mind-set:

> Wartime sacrifices to the emperor were quickly transformed into a mass movement of self-sacrifice for economic recovery. Living standards, leisure, and [other spending] were held down while industrialization and export promotion became holy writ [a sacred goal].[84]

In general, the Japanese, both in business and at home, tended to save more money than people in most other countries. Between 1961 and 1979, for example, the household savings rate in Japan ran between 18.2 and 22.1 percent of total earnings. The rate in the United States during the same period was 5.4 to 8.8 percent. Japanese savings usually went back into the economy in the form of investments, which further spurred financial growth.

Japan's Low Crime Rates

In this excerpt from his essay "National Security" in Japan: A Country Study, *scholar Ronald E. Dolan explains why modern Japan maintains crime rates lower than those of most other industrialized countries.*

"Two types of violations—larceny [theft] (64.7 percent of total violations) and negligent homicide or injury as a result of accidents (25.6 percent)—accounted for over 90 percent of criminal offenses in Japan in 1986. Major crimes occurred in Japan at a very low rate. Japan experienced 1.6 robberies per 100,000 population, compared with . . . 225.1 for the United States; and 1.4 murders per 100,000 population, compared with . . . 8.6 for the United States. . . . An important factor keeping crime low was the traditional emphasis on the individual as a member of groups to which he or she must not bring shame. Within these groups—family, friends, associates at work or school—a Japanese had social rights and obligations, derived valued emotional support, and met powerful expectations to conform. In 1990 these informal social sanctions continued to display remarkable potency despite competing values in a changing society. Other important factors keeping the crime rate low were the prosperous economy and a strict and effective weapons control law. Ownership of handguns was forbidden to the public, hunting rifles and ceremonial swords were registered with the police, and the manufacture and sale of firearms were regulated. . . . Despite Japan's status as a modern, urban nation—a condition linked by many criminologists to growing rates of crime—the nation did not suffer from steadily rising levels of criminal activity. Although crime continued to be higher in urban areas, in the 1980s rates of crime remained relatively constant nationwide, and rates of violent crime continued to decrease."

Still another factor contributing to the success of Japanese business and industry was the unique relationship between employers and their employees. In the postwar period, employers began guaranteeing their workers lifetime jobs. This policy helped the employers because it ensured a steady, loyal, and well-trained workforce. It helped the employees by ensuring steady work, company medical benefits, and a pension after retirement. According to W. Scott Morton:

> It is perceived by the workers to be in their own interest to do their best for the firm's fortunes. The managers, for their part, are expected to retain their employees and not dismiss them, even during a slump. There is therefore underemployment at intervals, but little unemployment. The larger firms provide free recreational facilities for their workers and, in some cases, free housing. Department stores offer classes gratis [free] to employees in flower arrangement, the tea ceremony and other accomplishments considered desirable for young women. Even small firms which do not boast expensive recreation opportunities still recognize the value of the bond between boss and worker. The owner and his wife may take a dozen employees with them for a couple of weeks' free holiday at the seashore.[85]

Third in the World

The net result of government support, good foreign trade relations, a stabilizing population, and diligent savings and work habits was a formidable period of economic growth in Japan lasting from the mid-1950s until the early 1990s. This so-called economic miracle was characterized by an annual GNP growth rate exceeding 10 percent between 1954 and 1967. In other words, in each of these years Japan's overall economic output was 10 percent bigger than it had been the year before—by far the largest economic growth rate in the world. By 1968, the nation's economy had surpassed in size that of West Germany, making Japan the third largest industrial power in the world after the United States and the Soviet Union.

And still the Japanese economy continued to grow. Between 1965 and 1970, the country more than doubled its production

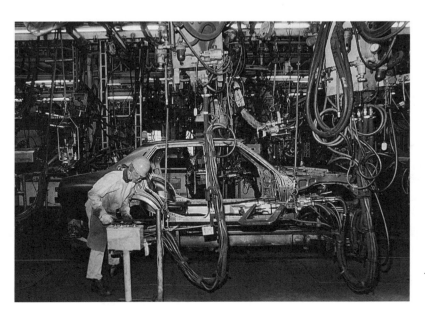

Workers, aided by sophisticated robotic machines, assemble an auto in the Nissan plant in Yokosuka. By the mid-1980s, Japanese factories like this one used large numbers of high-tech robots.

The opening day ceremonies of the 1964 summer Olympic Games in Tokyo. Japan's hosting of the games symbolized its new peaceful image.

of steel, from 41 million to 93 million tons. In the same short period the Japanese increased production of passenger cars from 696,000 to 3,178,000 and of television sets from 4.1 million to a staggering 13.8 million. In the 1970s Japan's output of cars, ships, and machine tools, as well as television sets and other electronic devices, continued to increase. This was because consumers in the United States and other Western countries had begun to perceive these Japanese products as cheaper, more efficient, and more durable than competing versions. Japan proudly showcased its image as an efficient, capable, and financially successful nation by hosting the 1964 Summer Olympics in Tokyo and the 1970 International Exposition in Osaka. These events, attended by representatives from around the world, were in a very real sense symbols of the new peaceful and economically viable Japan.

The late 1970s and early 1980s witnessed a new phase of the economic miracle thanks to advances in microelectronics made by Japanese researchers and firms. These innovations expanded the country's productivity still further by allowing Japan to capture a major share of the world computer and electronics markets. As a result of a range of global and domestic economic factors, the growth of Japan's economy slowed to about 5 percent a year in the late 1980s. Yet that figure was still formidable compared with growth in most other countries. The United States, for instance, had a growth rate of only 3.8 percent in the same period.

Effects on Society

The social effects of modern Japan's long economic boom were somewhat mixed. On the one hand, the country boasted modern cities, schools, roads, transportation systems, dams, and power plants. Most workers in large companies had employment security and received high wages and excellent benefits. As a result, they could afford a comfortable standard of living, comparable to that of upper-middle-class workers in Western countries. Many Japanese had extra money to spend on entertainment and luxuries even after paying the bills and saving for the future.

Also, because demand for workers in the bustling economy was so great, increasing numbers of women took jobs outside the home. By contributing to the support of their families, they gained independence

A TV Set in Every Home

Here, from an essay in Bunge's Japan: A Country Study, *scholar Jane T. Griffin describes modern Japanese television, which since the 1950s has grown into a national institution that reaches into nearly every Japanese home.*

"Television had attained virtually 100 percent penetration [of the nation's homes] by 1990, and only 1 percent of households were without a color television set, making Japan a major information society. Programming consisted of about 50 percent pure entertainment and nearly 25 percent cultural shows, the remainder being news reports and educational programs. There were two main broadcasting systems: the public NHK [Japan Broadcasting Corporation] and five private networks. . . . Samurai and *yakuza* (Japanese underworld) themes were now almost solely the provenance [constituted the main fare] of television, as were family life, [plentiful] on daytime soaps. The biggest hit of the 1980s overall was the television drama 'Oshin,' a tale of a mother's struggles and suffering. The longest-running series since 1981 was 'From the North Country,' in which a divorced father and his two children survive in the backwoods of Hokkaido. Criticisms continued concerning the vulgarity of some commercial programs, but these programs still appeared in the early 1990s. Major problems perceived [just as in American TV programming] were the high levels of violence and the lack of moral values in children's shows."

This worker at a Sony electronics factory is one of the many Japanese women employed in high-tech industries.

and respect, and helped to raise the status of Japanese women in general. Thus, wrote Morton in 1984:

> Today in Tokyo, it is possible for a Japanese woman to ask a bewildered tourist if he wants help, and to have a short conversation without any sense of restraint or awkwardness. This could never have happened in Japan before World War II. Women have emerged from the [feudal] status of vassals. . . .

One measure of increasing satisfaction Japanese women find in the control of their own lives is to be seen in a survey, in which the question posed to women was: If you could be born again, would you rather be as a man or a woman? The percentages answering "as a woman" were in 1958, 27%; in 1963, 36%; in 1973, 51%.[86]

But rapid economic growth and industrialization had their downsides, too. While employees of the big industrial companies did well, many other Japanese worked for small, usually nonindustrial, companies that could not afford to offer high wages and benefits. These workers, constituting almost two-thirds of the labor force, often had to put up with unsafe working conditions and substandard housing. Thus, much of the wealth accumulated in the economic boom remained in the hands of well-to-do industrialists and their lifetime employees, while Japan on the whole remained a low-wage country.

Industrial growth also came at the expense of the environment. By the 1970s and 1980s, says W. G. Beasley:

> Sulphurous air pollution [smog] had become a regular occurrence in the main urban centers. Water pollution, arising both from sewage disposal and industrial waste, had affected rivers, lakes, and coastal waters, especially enclosed areas, such as Tokyo Bay. . . . The effects on health included both mercury and cadmium poisoning, as well as a higher incidence of asthma [a respiratory ailment] in certain areas. . . . In several instances, victims of pollution-induced diseases successfully sued companies for compensation, only to face long legal battles on appeal.[87]

Facing a New Century

Eventually, Japan's economic boom ran its course. By 1993, the growth rate had slowed to less than 3 percent and unemployment had risen sharply. One major reason for this trend was a sluggish world economy, characterized by a decrease in demand for goods in general, including Japanese goods. Also, in the early 1990s several foreign manufacturers began to turn out products that competed well with Japanese versions. Some American car companies, for example, which had long suffered from competition with Toyotas, Subarus, and other Japanese exports, enjoyed rising sales and profits in 1993 and 1994. This slowing of economic growth has significantly affected Japan. According to Silk and Kono:

The protracted [long and continuing] slump has compelled many Japanese companies to "downsize" or close factories, and has shaken the lifetime employment system. Layoffs and rumors of layoffs to come are sending shock waves throughout the society.[88]

Japan's shrinking economy also had important political consequences. Voter dissatisfaction over the state of the economy, bolstered by charges of political corruption, finally brought down the once-popular Liberal Democratic Party. On July 18, 1993, the LDP was defeated by political forces led by statesman Morihiro Hosokawa. As the country's new prime minister, Hosokawa made economic and political reforms top priorities of his government. He promised to carry on the long struggle to make Japan the world's greatest economic giant, a scenario many

Japanese brokers display anxious expressions at news of falling stock prices in 1990. By 1993 the economic growth rate in Japan had dropped to less than 3 percent.

Government Payoffs and Dirty Money

Political corruption within the LDP-controlled Japanese government was a major factor in the party's 1993 defeat by reformers led by Morihiro Hosokawa. In this excerpt from their article "Sayonara, Japan Inc.," Leonard Silk and Tom Kono summarize the extent of the corruption.

"Japan's political corruption worsened in the 1980s as the 'bubble' economy provided business with a great deal of easy money to pay out [as bribes] to the politicians. Big corporations, with greater resources, generally outdid small ones. But the Recruit scandal, involving a relatively small company on the make [looking for illegal deals], forced prime minister Noboru Takeshita out of power and tarnished the reputations of former prime minister Yasuhiro Nakasone and then finance minister Kiichi Miyazawa. A less-subservient press exposed other cases of business-political corruption. The worst story was the Sagawa Kyubin scandal, which showed the close connection between LDP leaders and *yakuza*—organized crime groups. The public was shocked and angered to learn that Shin Kanemaru [a prominent public figure] . . . admitted that he had taken $4 million in illegal contributions. Emboldened prosecutors, who arrested Kanemaru on tax evasion charges in March 1993, found $50 million in cash and gold bars in his office. Corruption helped keep the Japanese market closed to foreign competitors. Unless the new political leaders rid themselves of Japan's post-war money politics—as Hosokawa [the prime minister in 1993] has promised to do—the Japanese economy will not be liberalized."

Well-known public figure Shin Kanemaru admitted to accepting millions of dollars worth of illegal contributions.

U.S. president Bill Clinton greets Japanese leader Morihiro Hosokawa in 1993. The meeting between these two self-styled political and social reformers marked a reaffirmation of the friendship between the two nations— once mortal enemies, now productive friends.

financial experts in the booming 1980s believed was a likely one.

But a rapidly changing world may make this goal increasingly difficult to attain. Japan's economic competitors grow yearly in number and strength, and the country's status and success in the future global economy are uncertain. Still, the Japanese remain and are likely to remain a major force in world affairs, thanks to their ingenuity, industriousness, and ability to adapt to change. These qualities, with which they so rapidly transformed Japan from a back-

ward feudal state into a modern one, and which guided their dramatic rise from the ashes of defeat in 1945 to the heights of economic success, are still their hallmarks. Edwin Reischauer remarks:

> The twenty-first century may not be "the Japanese century," as some non-Japanese have . . . proclaimed, but Japan may well be among the leaders—possibly even the preeminent leader—in finding solutions to the problems that mankind will face in the twenty-first century.[89]

Notes

Introduction: The Quest to Be Number One

1. Edwin O. Reischauer, *The Japanese*. Cambridge, MA: Harvard University Press, 1977
2. Reischauer, *The Japanese*.
3. Edward J. Lincoln, "International Economic Relations," in Ronald E. Dolan and Robert L. Worden, eds., *Japan: A Country Study*. Washington, DC: Library of Congress, 1992.
4. Robert J. Samuelson, "Japan as Number Two," *Newsweek*, December 6, 1993.

Chapter 1: Japan's Incredible Transformation: The Meiji Restoration

5. Edwin O. Reischauer, *Japan: The Story of a Nation*. New York: Knopf, 1970.
6. W. Scott Morton, *Japan: Its History and Culture*. New York: McGraw-Hill, 1984.
7. Quoted in W. G. Beasley, *The Modern History of Japan*. London: Weidenfeld and Nicolson, 1973.
8. Reischauer, *Japan: The Story of a Nation*.
9. Quoted in Morton, *Japan*.
10. Morton, *Japan*.
11. Robert L. Worden, "Historical Setting," in *Japan: A Country Study*.
12. Beasley, *The Modern History of Japan*.

Chapter 2: An Awakening Giant: Early Japanese Expansion

13. Edwin O. Reischauer, *Japan: Past and Present*. New York: Knopf, 1964.
14. Yamagata Aritomo, "Military Conscription Ordinance," quoted in William T. deBary, ed., *Sources of Japanese Tradition*. New York: Columbia University Press, 1964.
15. William T. de Bary, "Yamagata and the Army," in *Sources of Japanese Tradition*.
16. Oka Yoshitake, "Prologue," in Marlene J. Mayo, ed., *The Emergence of Imperial Japan: Self-Defense or Calculated Aggression?* Lexington, MA: Heath, 1970.
17. Quoted in Beasley, *The Modern History of Japan*.
18. Mutsu Munemitsu's diary, quoted in Mayo, *The Emergence of Imperial Japan*.
19. Morton, *Japan*.
20. Beasley, *The Modern History of Japan*.
21. Milton W. Meyer, *Japan: A Concise History*. Lanham, MD: Rowman and Littlefield, 1993.
22. Morton, *Japan*.

Chapter 3: From Admiration to Apprehension: Stepping onto the World Stage

23. Worden, "Historical Setting," in *Japan: A Country Study*.
24. Yamagata Aritomo, quoted in "China and the Twenty-One Demands," in deBary, *Sources of Japanese Tradition*.
25. Morton, *Japan*.
26. Reischauer, *Japan: The Story of a Nation*.
27. Worden, "Historical Setting," in *Japan: A Country Study*.
28. Quoted in George O. Totten, ed., *Democracy in Prewar Japan: Groundwork or Facade?* Lexington, MA: Heath, 1965.
29. Edwin O. Reischauer, "The Rise and Fall of Democratic Institutions in Prewar Japan," in Totten, *Democracy in Prewar Japan*.

30. Reischauer, "The Rise and Fall of Democratic Institutions in Prewar Japan," in Totten, *Democracy in Prewar Japan.*

31. Rinn-Sup Shinn, "Historical Setting," in Frederica M. Bunge, ed., *Japan: A Country Study.* Washington, DC: Library of Congress, 1982.

Chapter 4: Asia for the Asians: The Rise of the Japanese Militarists

32. Kita Ikki, *A Plan for the Reorganization of Japan,* quoted in de Bary, *Sources of Japanese Tradition.*

33. Meyer, *Japan.*

34. Quoted in Beasley, *The Modern History of Japan.*

35. Reischauer, *Japan: Past and Present.*

36. Henry L. Stimson, quoted in Louis L. Snyder, *The War: A Concise History, 1939–1945.* New York: Dell, 1960.

37. Quoted in Snyder, *The War.*

38. Snyder, *The War.*

39. Joseph C. Grew, *Ten Years in Japan.* New York: Simon and Schuster, 1944.

40. Reischauer, *Japan: Past and Present.*

41. Morton, *Japan.*

Chapter 5: Empire of the Sun: All-Out War in the Pacific

42. John Toland, *The Rising Sun: The Decline and Fall of the Japanese Empire, 1936–1945.* New York: Random House, 1970.

43. *Basic Plan for the Establishment of the Greater East Asia Coprosperity Sphere,* quoted in de Bary, *Sources of Japanese Tradition.*

44. Quoted in Snyder, *The War.*

45. Quoted in Snyder, *The War.*

46. Quoted in Toland, *The Rising Sun.*

47. Quoted in Toland, *The Rising Sun.*

48. Snyder, *The War.*

49. Toland, *The Rising Sun.*

50. Quoted in Snyder, *The War.*

51. Grew, *Ten Years in Japan.*

Chapter 6: The Flames of Defeat: Japan Risks and Loses All

52. Edwin P. Hoyt, *Japan's War: The Great Pacific Conflict, 1853–1952.* New York: McGraw-Hill, 1986.

53. Quoted in Toland, *The Rising Sun.*

54. Quoted in Snyder, *The War.*

55. Quoted in Hoyt, *Japan's War.*

56. Rikihei Inoguchi, *The Divine Wind,* quoted in Hans Dollinger, *The Decline and Fall of Nazi Germany and Imperial Japan.* New York: Bonanza Books, 1967.

57. Quoted in Toland, *The Rising Sun.*

58. Hoyt, *Japan's War.*

59. Mamoru Shigemitsu, *Japan and Her Destiny.* New York: Dutton, 1958.

60. Shigemitsu, *Japan and Her Destiny.*

61. Quoted in Dollinger, *The Decline and Fall.*

62. Quoted in Dollinger, *The Decline and Fall.*

63. John Hersey, *Hiroshima,* quoted in Dollinger, *The Decline and Fall.*

64. Quoted in Dollinger, *The Decline and Fall.*

65. Quoted in Toland, *The Rising Sun.*

66. Reischauer, *The Japanese.*

Chapter 7: My Enemy, My Friend: The Postwar Occupation

67. Robert Ward, quoted in Dolan and Worden, *Japan: A Country Study.*

68. Quoted in Toland, *The Rising Sun.*

69. Morton, *Japan.*

70. "Potsdam Proclamation," quoted in Harold S. Quigley and John E. Turner, *The New Japan: Government and Politics*. Minneapolis: University of Minnesota Press, 1956.

71. *Basic Initial Post-Surrender Directive*, quoted in Jon Livingston et al., eds., *The Japan Reader: Postwar Japan, 1945 to the Present*. New York: Random House, 1973.

72. Quoted in Dolan and Worden, *Japan: A Country Study*.

73. Letter from George Atcheson to President Harry Truman, November 5, 1945, quoted in Livingston, *The Japan Reader*.

74. Fukutake Tadashi, "Land Reform Laws," quoted in Livingston, *The Japan Reader*.

75. Quoted in Livingston, *The Japan Reader*.

76. Quoted in Morton, *Japan*.

77. Quoted in Morton, *Japan*.

78. Reischauer, *Japan: The Story of a Nation*.

79. Reischauer, *Japan: The Story of a Nation*.

80. Quoted in Snyder, *The War*.

Chapter 8: Economic Miracle: The Triumph of Modern Japan

81. Shinn, "Historical Setting," in Bunge, *Japan: A Country Study*.

82. Worden, "Historical Setting," in Dolan and Worden, *Japan: A Country Study*.

83. Reischauer, *The Japanese*.

84. Leonard Silk and Tom Kono, "Sayonara, Japan Inc.," in *Foreign Policy*, Winter 1993–1994.

85. Morton, *Japan*.

86. Morton, *Japan*.

87. Beasley, *The Modern History of Japan*.

88. Silk and Kono, "Sayonara, Japan Inc."

89. Reischauer, *The Japanese*.

For Further Reading

Gail Lee Bernstein, ed., *Recreating Japanese Women, 1660–1945*. Berkeley: University of California Press, 1991. A collection of essays by noted experts on Japanese culture. Each explores a typical role played by Japanese women in various historical periods. Advanced but worthwhile reading.

Jane Claypool, *Hiroshima and Nagasaki*. New York: Franklin Watts, 1984. A good summary of the events leading up to the nuclear destruction of these Japanese cities at the climax of World War II.

Martin Collcutt et al., *Cultural Atlas of Japan*. New York: Facts on File, 1988. This introduction to Japan, its geography, people, and historical periods, contains many informative maps, photos, and illustrations.

Bill Emmott, *The Sun Also Sets: The Limits to Japan's Economic Power*. New York: Times Books, 1989. Explains the main points of Japan's rise as an economic giant and discusses how the Japanese economy might fare in the future. Somewhat advanced reading.

Ronald Lewin, *The American Magic: Codes, Ciphers, and the Defeat of Japan*. New York: Farrar, Straus & Giroux, 1982. The fascinating story of how American cryptologists broke the Japanese codes, helping the country to achieve ultimate victory over the Japanese in World War II.

Don Nardo, *World War II: The War in the Pacific*. San Diego, CA: Lucent Books, 1991. An overview of the fateful clash between Japan and the United States in the Pacific sphere of the great global conflict.

Edwin O. Reischauer, *The Japanese Today: Continuity and Change*. Cambridge, MA: Harvard University Press, 1988. A fine synopsis of the major elements of modern Japanese society. Like Reischauer's other books, this is comprehensive, thoughtful, and easy to read.

Robert L. Reynolds, *Commodore Perry in Japan*. New York: American Heritage, 1963. Well-written account of Perry's expedition and how it opened Japan to the outside world.

Howard B. Schonberger, *Aftermath of War: Americans and the Remaking of Japan, 1945–1952*. Kent, OH: Kent State University Press, 1989. A detailed account of how the United States occupied and rebuilt Japan after World War II.

Works Consulted

W. G. Beasley, *The Modern History of Japan*. London: Weidenfeld and Nicolson, 1973. An excellent synopsis and analysis of modern Japanese history by one of the most respected scholars in the field.

T. A. Bisson, *Japan's War Economy*. New York: Macmillan, 1945. This technical report describing Japan's economic measures in the war was compiled at the end of the conflict by the Institute of Pacific Relations, a group that directed scientific studies of peoples and nations in the Pacific Ocean region.

Frederica M. Bunge, ed., *Japan: A Country Study*. Washington, DC: Library of Congress, 1982. This earlier version of the 1992 edition (see Dolan and Worden, eds., below) is also excellent and features many articles by different experts, in effect making this a different and equally useful book.

William T. de Bary, ed., *Sources of Japanese Tradition*. New York: Columbia University Press, 1964. An excellent two-volume collection of Japanese primary source documents from all historical periods up until the 1950s.

Ronald E. Dolan and Robert L. Worden, eds., *Japan: A Country Study*. Washington, DC: Library of Congress, 1992. A large, highly detailed overview of all aspects of Japanese civilization, from prehistory to the present. Includes useful maps, statistical tables, glossary, and bibliography.

Hans Dollinger, *The Decline and Fall of Nazi Germany and Imperial Japan*. New York: Bonanza Books, 1967. This large, valuable collection of speeches, letters, official documents, articles, and excerpts from books and other studies also contains hundreds of descriptive photos and informative lists of war data.

Joseph C. Grew, *Ten Years in Japan*. New York: Simon and Schuster, 1944. An informative and fascinating account of Japan in the 1930s, especially its politics, as seen through the collected diaries and private and official papers of the author, who served as U.S. ambassador to Japan from 1932 to 1942.

Larry Holyoke, "Firestorm Around the Fortress: Is Japan's Minister of Finance Saving or Strangling the Economy?" in *Business Week*, March 7, 1994. A discussion of some of Japan's latest economic problems.

Edwin P. Hoyt, *Japan's War: The Great Pacific Conflict, 1853–1952*. New York: McGraw-Hill, 1986. Hoyt carefully traces the growth of Japanese expansionism, beginning with the Meiji Restoration, and chronicles the collapse of Japan's empire in World War II. He also discusses the American occupation from 1945 to 1952.

Donald Keene, ed., *Modern Japanese Literature*. New York: Grove Press, 1956. An anthology of excerpts from Japanese stories, novels, and plays spanning the period 1868–1950.

Jon Livingston et al., eds., *The Japan Reader: Postwar Japan, 1945 to the Present*. New York: Random House, 1973. A large collection of articles, documents, speeches, and other primary sources relating to postwar Japan.

Roger Manvell, *Films and the Second World War*. New York: Dell, 1974. A very informative and readable synopsis of American, British, Japanese, German, and other films made for both propaganda and entertainment purposes during the war.

Marlene J. Mayo, ed., *The Emergence of Imperial Japan: Self-Defense or Calculated Aggression?* Lexington, MA: Heath, 1970. A collection of scholarly essays exploring Japanese expansion in the East Asian and Pacific spheres during the early twentieth century.

Milton W. Meyer, *Japan: A Concise History*. Lanham, MD: Rowman and Littlefield, 1993. A fine, up-to-date summary of Japanese history. Each chapter is broken down into separate discussions of politics, religion, culture, and so on.

Walter F. Mondale, "The U.S. and Japan: Working Together to Meet Economic Challenges," in *U.S. Department of State Dispatch*, December 27, 1993. The former vice president holds out great hope for the future of the two nations and their economies.

W. Scott Morton, *Japan: Its History and Culture*. New York: McGraw-Hill, 1984. One of the best general overviews of Japanese history, with plenty of coverage of literature and other cultural aspects.

Harold S. Quigley and John E. Turner, *The New Japan: Government and Politics*. Minneapolis: University of Minnesota Press, 1956. A detailed and well-written overview of Japan that focuses mainly on the years directly following World War II.

Edwin O. Reischauer, *Japan: Past and Present*. New York: Knopf, 1964. Respected scholar George Sansom said of this book, "I do not know of any short book on Japanese history which gives so much useful information in so brief and simple a form."

———, *Japan: The Story of a Nation*. New York: Knopf, 1970. Excellent summary of Japanese history and culture by the foremost American scholar in the field.

———, *The Japanese*. Cambridge, MA: Harvard University Press, 1977. This study of Japan uses the country's history to explain how modern Japanese act and think. In his preface, Reischauer comments, "I have . . . sought to achieve a wide focus on contemporary Japan as seen in the light of its whole past experience." He succeeds admirably.

Robert J. Samuelson, "Japan as Number Two," *Newsweek*, December 6, 1993. An editorial expressing the view that Japan will likely not end up dominating the world's economy in the future.

Mamoru Shigemitsu, *Japan and Her Destiny*. New York: Dutton, 1958. A moving account of Japan's military rise and fall told by a fine Japanese historian.

Leonard Silk and Tom Kono, "Sayonara, Japan Inc.," in *Foreign Policy*, Winter 1993–1994. A long and detailed discussion of modern Japanese politics, focusing on government corruption and how reforms might affect the country's future.

Louis L. Snyder, *The War: A Concise History, 1939–1945*. New York: Dell, 1960. One of the better general summaries of World War II, containing many useful and thought-provoking primary source quotes.

John Toland, *The Rising Sun: The Decline and Fall of the Japanese Empire, 1936–1945*. New York: Random House, 1970. This long, detailed, and dramatic book is one of the best studies available of the Pacific sphere in World War II. Well documented with many primary source quotes.

George O. Totten, ed., *Democracy in Prewar Japan: Groundwork or Facade?* Lexington, MA: Heath, 1965. A collection of scholarly essays exploring the rise and fall of democratic institutions in Japan in the early twentieth century.

Ezra Vogel, *Japan as Number One: Lessons for America*. Cambridge, MA: Harvard University Press, 1979. A broad-based discussion of Japanese social, economic, and political conditions since 1945.

Index

Picture Credits

About the Author

Don Nardo is an award-winning author whose more than fifty books cover a wide range of topics. His five studies of American wars include *The War of 1812, World War II: The War in the Pacific,* and *The Persian Gulf War,* and among his health-related works are *Medical Diagnosis, Anxiety and Phobias, Drugs and Sports,* and *Vitamins and Minerals.* Mr. Nardo has a degree in history; in addition to *Traditional Japan,* the companion volume to this book, his history studies include *Ancient Greece, The Roman Empire, Greek and Roman Theater,* and *Braving the New World.* In a related vein, he has written biographies of historical figures such as Cleopatra, Charles Darwin, Thomas Jefferson, H.G. Wells, and Franklin D. Roosevelt. His other writings include screenplays and teleplays, including work for Warner Brothers and ABC-Television. Mr. Nardo lives with his wife Christine on Cape Cod, Massachusetts.